ClearRevise

Edexcel GCSE
History 1HI0

Illustrated revision and practice

Option 31:
Weimar and Nazi Germany, 1918–39

Published by
PG Online Limited
The Old Coach House
35 Main Road
Tolpuddle
Dorset
DT2 7EW
United Kingdom

sales@pgonline.co.uk
www.clearrevise.com
www.pgonline.co.uk
2022

PG ONLINE

PREFACE

Absolute clarity! That's the aim.

This is everything you need to ace Paper 3 and beam with pride. Each topic is laid out in a beautifully illustrated format that is clear, approachable and as concise and simple as possible.

Each section of the specification is clearly indicated to help you cross-reference your revision. The checklist on the contents pages will help you keep track of what you have already worked through and what's left before the big day.

We have included worked exam-style questions with answers. There is also a set of exam-style questions at the end of each section for you to practise writing answers. You can check your answers against those given at the end of the book.

ACKNOWLEDGEMENTS

The questions in the ClearRevise textbook are the sole responsibility of the authors and have neither been provided nor approved by the examination board.

Every effort has been made to trace and acknowledge ownership of copyright. The publishers will be happy to make any future amendments with copyright owners that it has not been possible to contact. The publisher would like to thank the following companies and individuals who granted permission for the use of their images in this textbook.

Design and artwork: Jessica Webb, Mike Bloys / PG Online Ltd
Graphics / images: © Shutterstock

French soldiers at Ruhr © Everett Collection / Shutterstock
Bauhaus era building © meunierd / Shutterstock
Nazi election posters © Everett Collection / Shutterstock
Nazi parade © Everett Collection / Shutterstock
Road construction © Everett Collection / Shutterstock
Sachsenhausen image © Everett Collection / Shutterstock

Stresemann portrait © Everett Collection / Shutterstock
Hitler portrait © Everett Collection / Shutterstock
Gestapo officers © Everett Collection / Shutterstock
Nazi poster © Everett Collection / Shutterstock
WW2 German Nazi SS black cap © Militarist / Shutterstock
Marlene Dietrich in Blonde Venus © emka74 / Shutterstock

Images on pages 5, 6, 15, 18, 19, 21, 22, 29, 41, 46, 52, 57 © Alamy
Freikorps poster on p7: Gipkens, Julius E. F., 1883- artist. Schütz eure Heimat! Tretet bei dem Freikorps Hülsen [graphic] / Gipkens. Berlin : Hollerbaum & Schmidt, [1918]
The Weimar Republic, Eberhard Kolb, Copyright (© 1984). Reproduced by permission of Taylor & Francis Group. Reproduced with permission of the Licensor through PLSclear.
The Rise and Fall of the Third Reich. Reprinted by permission of Abner Stein on behalf of Don Congdon Associates © 1960, renewed 1988 by William L. Shirer
The Gestapo, Jacques Delarue. Reproduced with permission from Pen & Sword Books.
The Nazi Impact on a German Village, Walter Rinderle and Bernard Norling (c) 1993. Reproduced with permission of the Licensor through the Copyright Clearance Centre.
From Mothers in the Fatherland: Women, the Family and Nazi Politics by Claudia Koonz; © 1986 by Claudia Koonz.
Gupta, C. (1991). Politics of Gender: Women in Nazi Germany. Economic and Political Weekly, 26(17), WS40–WS48.
Lee, Stephen, Heinemann Secondary History Project Weimar and Nazi Germany Core Book, ©1996 Reprinted by permission of Pearson Education Limited
Democracy and Nazism, Robert Whitfield, copyright (© 2015). Reproduced with permission of the Licensor through PLSclear.

First edition 2022   10 9 8 7 6 5 4 3 2 1
A catalogue entry for this book is available from the British Library
ISBN: 978-1-910523-42-1
Contributor: Andrew Wallace
Copyright © PG Online 2022
All rights reserved

THE SCIENCE OF REVISION

Illustrations and words

Research has shown that revising with words and pictures doubles the quality of responses by students.[1] This is known as 'dual-coding' because it provides two ways of fetching the information from our brain. The improvement in responses is particularly apparent in students when they are asked to apply their knowledge to different problems. Recall, application and judgement are all specifically and carefully assessed in public examination questions.

Retrieval of information

Retrieval practice encourages students to come up with answers to questions.[2] The closer the question is to one you might see in a real examination, the better. Also, the closer the environment in which a student revises is to the 'examination environment', the better. Students who had a test 2–7 days away did 30% better using retrieval practice than students who simply read, or repeatedly reread material. Students who were expected to teach the content to someone else after their revision period did better still.[3] What was found to be most interesting in other studies is that students using retrieval methods and testing for revision were also more resilient to the introduction of stress.[4]

Ebbinghaus' forgetting curve and spaced learning

Ebbinghaus' 140-year-old study examined the rate at which we forget things over time. The findings still hold true. However, the act of forgetting facts and techniques and relearning them is what cements them into the brain.[5] Spacing out revision is more effective than cramming – we know that, but students should also know that the space between revisiting material should vary depending on how far away the examination is. A cyclical approach is required. An examination 12 months away necessitates revisiting covered material about once a month. A test in 30 days should have topics revisited every 3 days – intervals of roughly a tenth of the time available.[6]

Summary

Students: the more tests and past questions you do, in an environment as close to examination conditions as possible, the better you are likely to perform on the day. If you prefer to listen to music while you revise, tunes without lyrics will be far less detrimental to your memory and retention. Silence is most effective.[5] If you choose to study with friends, choose carefully – effort is contagious.[7]

1.   Mayer, R. E., & Anderson, R. B. (1991). Animations need narrations: An experimental test of dual-coding hypothesis. *Journal of Education Psychology*, (83)4, 484–490.

2.   Roediger III, H. L., & Karpicke, J.D. (2006). Test-enhanced learning: Taking memory tests improves long-term retention. *Psychological Science*, 17(3), 249–255.

3.   Nestojko, J., Bui, D., Kornell, N. & Bjork, E. (2014). Expecting to teach enhances learning and organisation of knowledge in free recall of text passages. *Memory and Cognition*, 42(7), 1038–1048.

4.   Smith, A. M., Floerke, V. A., & Thomas, A. K. (2016) Retrieval practice protects memory against acute stress. *Science*, 354(6315), 1046–1048.

5.   Perham, N., & Currie, H. (2014). Does listening to preferred music improve comprehension performance? *Applied Cognitive Psychology*, 28(2), 279–284.

6.   Cepeda, N. J., Vul, E., Rohrer, D., Wixted, J. T. & Pashler, H. (2008). Spacing effects in learning a temporal ridgeline of optimal retention. *Psychological Science*, 19(11), 1095–1102.

7.   Busch, B. & Watson, E. (2019), *The Science of Learning*, 1st ed. Routledge.

CONTENTS

MARK ALLOCATIONS

Green mark allocations[1] on answers to in-text questions through this guide help to indicate where marks are gained within the answers. A bracketed '1' e.g. [1] = one valid point worthy of a mark. There are often many more points to make than there are marks available so you have more opportunities to max out your answers than you may think.

Higher mark questions require extended responses. Marks are not given as the answers should be marked as a whole in accordance with the levels on **pages 60-62**.

Understanding the specification reference tabs

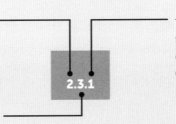

This number refers to the key topic. In this example, *Hitler's rise to power, 1919–33.*

This number refers to the bullet point. In this example, *The growth of unemployment.*

This number refers to the subtopic. In this example, *The growth in support for the Nazis, 1929–32.*

2.3.1

THE EXAM

There are six questions in Paper 3 — Modern Depth Study. The questions follow the same format every year, so make sure you're familiar with them before the big day.

Q1 'Give two things you can infer from Source A about...'

This question tests your ability to read between the lines of a source to make an inference. You then have to support your inference by quoting or paraphrasing the source or by making a valid comment about the source or its content. The question is worth 4 marks and you have to make two inferences, so your answer doesn't need to be longer than a couple of lines for each inference.

Q2 'Explain why...'

This question tests your understanding of **causation** (why something happened). There will be two stimulus points to help you, but to get top marks, you need to include information that goes beyond these stimulus points. This question is worth 12 marks, and a detailed response is expected. To score at the highest level, you have to give an analytical explanation with a logical and sustained line of reasoning. You also have to support your explanation with accurate and relevant information.

Q3 (a) 'How useful are Sources B and C for an enquiry into...'

This question tests your ability to evaluate two sources and judge how useful they are for an enquiry (a historical investigation). The sources will be provided in the exam, and you need to think about the sources' provenance: when the sources were created, who created them, why the sources were created and what the sources contain. You should evaluate the usefulness of the sources, as well as any limitations that they have, for example, a written source could be one-sided, or a photograph could have been staged. This question is worth 8 marks, and you need to evaluate both the sources to get top marks.

Q3 (b) 'Study Interpretations 1 and 2. What is the main difference between the views?'

This question tests your ability to analyse two interpretations that will be supplied in the exam. An interpretation is a historian's opinion of historical events. You are asked to show how the overall message in two separate interpretations differ. This question is only worth 4 marks, but you still need to make sure you back up your points with evidence from the interpretations.

Q3 (c) 'Suggest one reason why Interpretations 1 and 2 give different views about...'

This question uses the same interpretations as Q3 (b). You need to suggest one reason why they might differ, for example they may have chosen to focus on different details or used different sources to justify their opinions. You can use the sources from Q3 (a) to help support your answer but you don't have to.

Q3 (d) 'How far do you agree with the Interpretation about...'

This question asks you to look at Interpretation 2 and explain how far you agree with it. You need to use Interpretation 1 (which you already know disagrees with it) and your own knowledge to write a detailed explanation showing where you agree and where you do not agree with Interpretation 2. You must reach a conclusion on whether you agree more than you disagree. This conclusion should include an overall judgment based on a logical and supported line of reasoning.

There are 4 marks available for spelling, punctuation and grammar. Make sure you carefully re-read your answer at the end and clearly correct any errors.

TOPICS FOR PAPER 3,
MODERN DEPTH STUDY

Option 31:
Weimar and Nazi Germany, 1918–39

Information about Paper 3

Written exam: 1 hour 20 minutes
30% of total GCSE
52 marks

Specification coverage

Key topic 1: The Weimar Republic 1918–29

Key topic 2: Hitler's rise to power, 1919–33

Key topic 3: Nazi control and dictatorship, 1933–39

Key topic 4: Life in Nazi Germany, 1933–39

Questions

The paper is divided into two sections:

Section A: One question based on a single source and another question that assesses knowledge and understanding.

Section B: A single four-part question, based on two sources and two interpretations.

You must answer all of the questions.

THE ORIGINS OF THE REPUBLIC, 1918–19

The Weimar Republic was the name given to the German system of government between 1919–1933.

Legacy of the First World War

In 1918, World War I was coming to an end. The war had taken its toll on Germany.

Almost 2 million soldiers had died, and 4.2 million were wounded. The war had devastated civilians too. A naval blockade by the Allies (France, Britain, and USA) between 1914–19 prevented supplies from reaching Germany. This led to starvation, and 500,000 German civilians died.

Germany was in massive debt – it owed three times as much in 1918 as it had in 1914. The German wartime government had issued War Bonds (bonds purchased by the public to finance wars) and had overspent their budget.

This led to unrest across Germany, including the Kiel mutiny, a large-scale revolt by German sailors which triggered the revolution.

The revolution

The German people were hungry, angry and on the brink of civil war.

October 1918

Strikes and riots took place in German cities, including Hamburg, Stuttgart, and Kiel. Many cities were run by workers', soldiers', and sailors' councils ('Soviets').

November 1918

The strikes and riots spread to Berlin. There was a large protest, and the **SPD** (Social Democratic Party) demanded that the Kaiser (German emperor) abdicate.

9 November 1918   Abdication of the Kaiser

On 9th November 1918, Kaiser Wilhelm lost the support of his ministers and the army, partly due to the unrest across Germany. He abdicated and fled to Holland on 10th November.

The abdication of the Kaiser created a power vacuum in Germany, and two different socialist parties announced a German Republic. **Friedrich Ebert**, the leader of the SPD, became Chancellor, the **Reichstag** (parliament) was suspended, and a temporary government, the **Council of People's Representatives**, was set up.

Abdicate means to step down as a ruling monarch.

11 November 1918   The armistice

Ebert's representative signed an **armistice** (truce) to end the war. It led to the Treaty of Versailles on 28th June 1919 (see **page 4**). The new German government felt they had to agree to the armistice since German civilians were starving, and the war had caused millions of casualties. Despite this, some right-wing Germans didn't agree with the truce and thought Germany could still win the war. They called the politicians who agreed to the armistice the **November Criminals**.

THE SETTING UP OF THE WEIMAR REPUBLIC

In 1919, the Council of People's Representatives organised elections to decide how Germany was going to be run.

Beginnings of the Weimar Republic

The monarchy had been abolished and Germany was now a democracy. Elections were organised so the public could have their say in the new republic.

January 1919

Elections had 82% voter turn-out. Centre parties (neither left- nor right-wing) performed well. The SPD won 38% of the vote and were the largest party.

February 1919

The **National Assembly** met to draw up a new **Constitution** for Germany.

July 1919

The new Constitution was agreed, and the **Weimar Republic** was born.

Strengths

- The new government was based on **Proportional Representation** (PR). This meant seats were given to political parties according to the percentage of votes they received. This was fairer.
- Laws needed to pass from the Reichstag through the Reichsrat. This meant laws were reviewed and authorised by multiple groups.
- The government was no longer under the control of a single leader. Power now belonged to voters.

Weaknesses

- PR led to multiple parties in the Reichstag which meant it was very difficult to reach an agreement on some issues.
- **Article 48** allowed the President to override and suspend the Reichstag. He could pass laws unchecked.
- If the public voted for extreme parties, there was a chance that they might be elected.

The Weimar Constitution

The Constitution introduced a new system of government:

The President

- Had the most power.
- Elected every 7 years by the German people.
- Could choose the Chancellor and direct the army.
- Could suspend the Reichstag, call elections, and waive the Constitution.

The Chancellor

- Leader of largest party.
- Elected every four years.
- In charge of the day-to-day running of government.
- Could choose Cabinet ministers.

Parliament

Elected every four years, and had two parliamentary bodies:

Reichstag

Controlled finances and could propose laws.

Reichsrat

Less powerful, but checked the Reichstag. Could stop laws.

REASONS FOR THE EARLY UNPOPULARITY OF THE WEIMAR REPUBLIC

In June 1919, the Weimar Government signed the **Treaty of Versailles**, a peace treaty drawn up after the First World War. The Treaty was written by the Allies (Britain, France and the USA), and Germany had no say in its terms.

Key terms of the Treaty of Versailles

The Weimar Government didn't want to sign, but they had little choice. The German people felt humiliated by the treaty and betrayed by those who agreed to it. The German people saw it as a **diktat**, something that had been forced on Germany.

Military cuts

The German army was limited to 100,000 men. The navy was limited to 6 battleships, 6 cruisers, 12 destroyers and 12 torpedo boats. The German army was not allowed to possess submarines or aircraft. No military forces were allowed in the 'demilitarised' German Rhineland on France's border.

Impact

A reduced army and navy made Germany feel vulnerable.

Article 231 — War Guilt Clause

Germany had to accept blame for starting the war. This clause meant all the other terms were legitimised.

Impact

Germans resented the accusation they were responsible.

Loss of land

Alsace-Lorraine was lost to France, and Eupen and Malmedy to Belgium. Danzig, in East Prussia (which was now separated from the rest of Germany), was declared a 'free' port. The coal-rich Saar was to be governed by France for 15 years. Germany lost all 11 of its colonies overseas. These were given to the victorious countries as 'mandates' (territories for them to look after).

Impact

Germany lost its empire. Germans who lived in the parts of Germany lost to Europe now technically lived in a different country.

Reparations

Reparations were compensation payments for the cost of the war. These were set in 1921, and Germany had to repay £132 billion gold marks (approximately £284 billion today) to the victorious nations.

Impact

The payments were enormous and would have a lasting impact on Germany's economy.

The 'stab in the back' theory

The collapse of the German Empire, the signing of the armistice and the Treaty of Versailles led to conspiracy theories amongst some Germans. These theories were known as **Dolchstoss** ('dagger stab legend'). The army had not lost on the battlefield; it had been 'stabbed in the back' by disloyalty at home in Germany.

Reasons for support of conspiracy theories

- Defeat in World War I had damaged national pride and Germans wanted to blame someone.

- Some Germans didn't believe the German army had lost because there hadn't been any combat on German soil. They thought that something else must have caused the defeat.

- Others felt that the war could have just as easily swung back in Germany's favour, and that the war had ended prematurely.

This cartoon shows a German soldier being stabbed in the back by someone with a Star of David on their cuff. The Star of David is a Jewish symbol.

Scapegoats

Different groups were blamed for the German defeat.
- Army generals blamed parliament, politicians, and the government.

- Some Germans who held **antisemitic** beliefs (beliefs that were prejudiced against Jews) thought that Jewish people were responsible.

- Nationalists blamed socialism, communism, and trade unions for the defeat.

Significance   Dolchstoss

The stab-in-the-back theories highlight the tensions between the Weimar Republic and the German population, as well as demonstrating pre-existing antisemitic feeling. When Hitler rose to power, he used Dolchstoss in his speeches to gain support from the public and discredit the Weimar Government.

CHALLENGES TO THE REPUBLIC FROM LEFT AND RIGHT

Both left- and right-wing political groups challenged the authority of the Weimar Republic.

The left: Spartacists

The **Spartacists**, led by Karl Liebknecht and Rosa Luxemburg, were a communist organisation who believed that wealth and power should be spread evenly amongst the German population.

1919   Spartacist Revolt

The Spartacists wanted to overthrow the Weimar Government and replace it with local councils run by soldiers and workers. They had been inspired by the 1917 Revolution in Russia which had toppled the royal family and they were prepared to use violent methods to achieve their aims.

In January 1919, the Spartacists mobilised 100,000 workers to go on strike in Berlin and seized control of newspaper and communication buildings. However, many of those involved in the revolt were frustrated that the Spartacists didn't know what to do next.

Chancellor Ebert had to rely on the **Freikorps** (see **page 7**) to dispel the uprising, and over 100 workers were killed. The Spartacist leaders were arrested and murdered by the Freikorps. The uprising and the level of violence led to a hatred between the Communists and the Social Democrats.

Source A:

The shameful actions of Karl Liebknecht and Rosa Luxemburg have damaged all that has been achieved since the Kaiser was overthrown. The people of Germany must not sit quiet for one minute longer while these brutal beasts and their followers paralyse the activities of the government and encourage more and more people to rebellion.

From a newspaper which supported the Weimar Government, January 1919

The German Communist Party was known as the **KPD** (Kommunistische Partei Deutschlands).

1. Give **two** things you can infer from Source A about attitudes towards the Spartacists in 1919.   [4]

     1. *What I can infer:* I can infer that their actions were not supported by most German people. [1]

        Details in the source that tell me this: The text says "the people of Germany must not sit quiet for one minute longer". [1]

     2. *What I can infer:* I can infer that the Spartacists were violent. [1]

        Details in the source that tell me this: The writer describes Liebknecht and Luxembourg as "brutal beasts". [1]

The right: Freikorps

The **Freikorps** were a right-wing group of ex-soldiers who believed in nationalism (loyalty to Germany). Ebert tried to disband the Freikorps because they were becoming too powerful, but they refused.

A recruitment poster for the Freikorps which says: "Protect your homeland! Enlist in the Freikorps."

Key events of the Kapp Putsch

In March 1920, around 5,000 members of the Freikorps marched on Berlin. They wanted to overthrow the Weimar Government and create a new right-wing government. Ebert ordered the German army to stop them, but the army refused to obey orders because they didn't want to open fire on fellow soldiers.

The Weimar Government fled, and Dr Wolfgang Kapp, the leader of the revolt (known as the **Kapp Putsch**), was declared head of a new government. The Weimar Government ordered workers in Berlin to strike, and Berlin was brought to a standstill. Kapp fled, and the putsch collapsed. The Weimar Government was restored four days after the putsch began.

Putsch is the German word for 'revolt'.

Further unrest

Between 1919–22, left- and right-wing groups caused more turmoil. There were nearly 400 assassinations, including Matthias Erzberger, a left-wing politician who had signed the Treaty of Versailles. He was gunned down while on holiday by a member of a nationalist organisation. Most murders were of members of the left by supporters of the right, but judges tended to be sympathetic to the right, meaning punishment was light.

There were soon several armed groups on the streets:

- **Stahlhelm** a right-wing group of war veterans named for their steel helmets.

- **Rotfrontkaempfer** (Red Front Fighters) a left-wing group associated with the KPD.

- **Reichsbanner Schwarz-Rot-Gold** (Black-Red-Gold Flagbearers) a moderate group loyal to the SPD and the new Republic.

SPD stands for *Sozialdemokratische Partei Deutschlands* (Social Democratic Party of Germany).

2. Explain why the Weimar Government faced difficulties in the years 1918–22.

You may use the following in your answer:

- the legacy of the First World War
- the powers of the government

You **must** also use information of your own. [12]

Your answer may include:

The legacy of the First World War:

- *Germany had lost 2 million soldiers and 4.2 million were wounded. This meant that the German workforce was weakened, and industry took a long time to recover.*
- *The naval blockade continued until 1919, so food shortages led to a starving and malnourished population.*
- *Conspiracy theories about Germany's defeat in the First World War (Dolchstoss) caused tensions between the government and the public. The Weimar politicians who had signed the armistice were nicknamed the November Criminals.*

The powers of the government:

- *Proportional representation meant that there was a lot of disagreement between different political parties, and it was difficult for the government to reach an agreement on issues.*

Treaty of Versailles:

- *The Weimar Government had been forced to sign the Treaty of Versailles by the Allies. The treaty was very severe, and many Germans felt that they had been humiliated and betrayed by the Weimar politicians who had agreed to it.*
- *War Guilt clause meant many felt betrayed by the government so the Weimar Government lost support.*
- *Germany had agreed to pay reparations to the Allies. A figure of £6.6 billion was set in 1921. This would be an enormous financial burden for the country.*

Challenges from the left and the right:

- *Both left-wing and right-wing political parties challenged the authority of the Weimar Government which led to political unrest. The Spartacists led a revolt in 1919 and the right-wing led the Kapp Putsch. Both these uprisings attempted to overthrow the Weimar Government.*

This question should be marked in accordance with the levels-based mark scheme on page 60.

Make sure your answer to this question is in paragraphs and full sentences. Bullet points have been used in this example answer to suggest some information you could include.

To get top marks, you need to include information other than the bullet points in the question.

THE CHALLENGES OF 1923

Germany began paying reparations set out by the Treaty of Versailles. Germany was crippled by the first repayment and failed to pay some instalments.

French occupation of the Ruhr

By December 1922, Germany was unable to pay reparations. In January 1923, French and Belgian troops **occupied the Ruhr** (Germany's main industrial area), and began to take control of mines, factories, and transport to collect reparations themselves. The German government ordered **passive resistance**. They knew their reduced army was no match for the French, so German workers went on strike instead, and the French brought in their own labour force.

French soldiers with a machine gun during the occupation of the Ruhr in 1923.

Effects of the occupation of the Ruhr

Germany's economic situation worsened as debt piled up and Germany lost control of a major industrial area. The government continued to pay strikers, and compensated owners for lost income, which added to the nation's debt. As a result, prices went up, so the government printed more money as a way of meeting payments. This led to **inflation** (a rise in prices, and a fall in the value of money).

Hyperinflation

By 1923, this cycle of price inflations became **hyperinflation**.

People began to lose faith in money as prices rose rapidly.

Prices continued to rise. Notes were used as toys or wallpaper.

Money became worthless, which was devastating for people with life savings. People swapped goods and services instead.

Internationally, no one wanted to trade with Germany which led to food shortages.

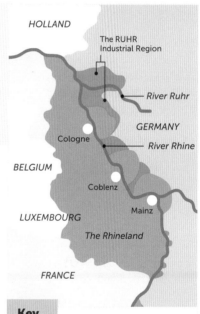

HOLLAND

The RUHR Industrial Region

River Ruhr

GERMANY

Cologne

River Rhine

BELGIUM

Coblenz

Mainz

LUXEMBOURG

The Rhineland

FRANCE

Key

After 1918: Occupied by Allied forces after the armistice.

January 1923: Occupied by French and Belgian forces.

Some people benefitted from hyperinflation. Loans became easier to pay off and the Black Market flourished.

REASONS FOR ECONOMIC RECOVERY

Many saw **Gustav Stresemann** as the saviour of Germany in the 1920s. He was Chancellor only from August to November 1923, but he kept the post of Foreign Minister until his death in 1929.

Stresemann and economic recovery

End to passive resistance

Stresemann's priority was to end the occupation of the Ruhr. In 1923 he called off passive resistance and strikers went back to work, which eased tensions between Germany, France, and Belgium, and meant the government was no longer paying workers' wages. Although the occupation continued until 1925, Stresemann's actions helped stabilise the economy.

Currency

Stresemann restored people's faith in paper money. He introduced the **Rentenmark**, a new currency, backed by a new state-owned bank. Value was tied to land, so it had 'real' value. This was replaced by the **Reichsmark** in 1924. This currency gained international trust and made trade possible again.

Dawes Plan

In 1924, Stresemann signed the **Dawes Plan**, which:

- Reduced reparations (in the short-term) to £50 million per year.
- Agreed a more realistic timeline of payments for the reparations.
- Agreed that the **USA** would **loan** Germany £40 million to invest in rebuilding its industries.

Consequences of the Dawes Plan

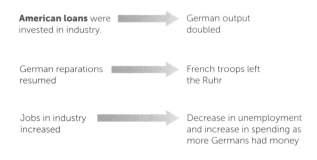

American loans were invested in industry. → German output doubled

German reparations resumed → French troops left the Ruhr

Jobs in industry increased → Decrease in unemployment and increase in spending as more Germans had money

Young Plan

In 1929, the **Young Plan** was agreed between Germany and the Allies. It reduced reparations even further from £6.6 billion down to £2 billion. Repayments were rescheduled over 59 more years to 1988. This further improved confidence in Germany's economy, as taxes came down and job opportunities increased in growing industries. The government held a referendum (public vote) on the Young Plan and 85% of Germans voted in favour of the plan.

Those who voted against the Young Plan thought it would be a burden on the future and it angered those who resented the Treaty of Versailles.

In the end, the Young Plan came to nothing. America recalled the loans after the Wall Street Crash (page 24) and the German economy was devastated and reparation payments stopped.

THE IMPACT OF STRESEMANN'S ACHIEVEMENTS ABROAD

Stresemann's foreign policy led to three other agreements which improved confidence in Germany at home and abroad.

Stresemann's foreign policy

1925 Locarno Pact

An agreement signed by Germany, France, Britain, Belgium, and Italy to maintain the western borders of Europe. It also agreed to the permanent demilitarisation of the Rhineland. Negotiations began to allow Germany to join the League of Nations.

⊕ Germany was being treated on equal terms, not dictated to.

⊖ The Locarno Pact reinforced some of the terms from the Treaty of Versailles, such as the demilitarisation of the Rhineland, which angered some extremists.

1926 League of Nations

Germany became a member of the League, which had been founded in 1919 to keep peace. Germany was now able to contribute to international issues alongside the victors of World War I.

⊕ Germany was given more say in international affairs and had more respect abroad.

⊖ The League had been set up following the end of World War I, and some felt that Germany joining the League was an extension of the betrayal of the Treaty of Versailles.

1928 Kellogg-Briand Pact

Germany and 61 other nations signed an anti-war agreement.

⊕ Germany was treated as an equal with the 61 other nations, which proved the other countries involved in the pact trusted Germany.

⊖ It didn't reverse any of the military restrictions which had been placed on Germany following the Treaty of Versailles.

Results

Stresemann's efforts to get Germany international acceptance had a tremendous impact on the government's ability to maintain domestic stability. German voters backed moderate politicians rather than extreme left- or right-wing parties.

Changes in the Presidency

Ebert died in 1925. The new President, Field Marshal **Paul von Hindenburg**, was popular. He was a figure of calm authority, and a respected war leader. He brought together those who believed in the Weimar Republic, as well as those who had supported the Kaiser.

Source B:

In such co-operation the basis of the future must be sought. The great majority of the German people stands firm for such a peace as this. Relying on this will for peace, we set our signature to this treaty. It is to introduce a new era of cooperation among the nations. It is to close the seven years that followed the War, by a time of real peace, upheld by the will of responsible and far-seeing statesmen.

Gustav Stresemann, at the official signing of the Locarno Pact, December 1925.

Source C:

Our representatives are little men who are no match for patronising British diplomacy. Like the chancellor and ambitious busybodies who must have their fingers in every pie. Like Stresemann, the man of general distrust, but it seems impossible to get rid of him... My opposition to our foreign policy is generally known.

General Hans von Seeckt, Commander-in-Chief of the German Army in a letter to his sister, April 1926

Study Sources B and C. How useful are Sources B and C for an enquiry into the success of Stresemann's Foreign Policy in 1924–29?

Explain your answer using Sources B and C and your knowledge of the historical context.   [8]

Your answer may include:

Source B:

- *Source B is useful because it suggests the German people are supportive of the Locarno Pact. Stresemann needed popular support to avoid a return to the political troubles of 1919-23.*

- *Source B provides evidence that Stresemann put Germany on a global stage, as he is addressing international leaders. This agrees with my own knowledge that the Locarno Pact was signed by Britain, France, Belgium, and Italy.*

- *The source is useful because of its provenance. Stresemann was the architect of the Pact and was given a platform to address the other nations involved with the Pact. It would have received widespread coverage in the press and provided proof to Germans of the success of Stresemann's foreign policy.*

- *Its usefulness is limited by its lack of objectivity since it is from Stresemann himself and he would have been keen to show that his foreign policy was a success.*

Source C:

- *Source C is also useful because it suggests Stresemann did not have the support of senior members of the army, which he would need to make his foreign policy successful. They felt Stresemann was weakening Germany, and that he was being manipulated by Britain.*

- *This agrees with my own knowledge that Stresemann had pushed Germany into agreement with Britain over Western European borders. He would later involve Germany in signing the anti-war Kellogg-Briand Pact of over 60 nations.*

- *Source C is useful because of its provenance. The author is a high-ranking and influential member of the German military. He wrote this at the height of Stresemann's foreign policies.*

- *It would not have been written for publication so it's unlikely that he would say things to his sister which weren't true. As such, it helps a reader to come to a balanced judgement on the success of Stresemann's policies.*

This question should be marked in accordance with the levels-based mark scheme on page 61.

Make sure your answer to this question is in paragraphs and full sentences. Bullet points have been used in this example answer to suggest some information you could include.

CHANGES IN THE STANDARD OF LIVING

Germany's economy gradually improved between 1924–29. This allowed the government to make social changes which improved the lives of many Germans.

The Golden Age

The period between 1924–29 is known as the Golden Age of the Weimar Republic.

- **Wages** rose steadily. In 1927, they rose by 9%. In 1928, they rose by 12%.
- 2 million homes were built between 1924–31. This created more **housing**, and more construction jobs.
- **The Unemployment Insurance Act of 1927** taxed 3% of workers' wages to provide unemployment and sickness benefits of 60 Marks per week. This meant the unemployed had more security and protection.
- The number of students in higher education rose by 50% from 1914–28.

- Unemployment fell to 1.3 million by 1928.
- Working hours were shortened.
- Homelessness fell by 60% by 1928.

Continuity   The middle classes

The middle classes didn't benefit as much from wage rises and welfare benefits compared to the working classes. Unemployment among the middle class remained high, and this created some resentment towards the Weimar Government.

CHANGES IN THE POSITION OF WOMEN

Compared to other countries at the time, women in the Weimar Republic had significant rights and freedoms in **work**, **politics** and **leisure**.

Women's rights — in theory

The Weimar Constitution (see **page 3**) gave women:

- equal rights with men
- equal rights within marriage
- equality at work, and in employment
- the right to vote
- the right to stand in elections.

Women's rights — in reality

Although the Constitution promoted equality, this wasn't always the case. By 1925, women made up 36% of the workforce, but this was only in-line with 1918 levels. The gender wage gap was 33%.

Women were still expected to give up work once they married, and very few found their way into high profile professions, such as judges. However, some women moved into more vocational professions, such as teaching, and the number of female doctors doubled from 1925–32. There were also plenty of women working in shops and offices.

By 1932, 112 women had been elected to the Reichstag, but this represented fewer than 10% of Reichstag members.

Divorce rates doubled in the 1920s and birth rates fell by 50%.

New Women

The Weimar Republic saw the rise of **New Women**. They were often young, single, and lived in the cities. New Women:

- dressed as they wished, and wore jewellery
- went to bars and nightclubs
- enjoyed sexual freedom
- smoked and drank alcohol

Cinemas embraced New Women by creating strong 'femme fatale' characters (right).

Difference	Attitudes to women in society

Changes to women's rights were not embraced by traditionalists. They felt these new freedoms threatened the traditional family structure and German values.

Source D:

Women began to cut an entirely new figure. A new economic figure who went out into public economic life as an independent worker or wage-earner entering the free market that had up until then been free only for men. A new political figure who appeared in the parties and parliaments, at demonstrations and gatherings. A new physical figure who not only cut her hair and shortened her skirts but began to emancipate herself altogether from the physical limitations of being female.

An article published in 1933, by Alice Rühle-Gerstel

Source E:
A cartoon published in a satirical German magazine in 1921

How useful are Sources D and E for an enquiry into the changes in the position of women during the Weimar Republic?

Explain your answer using Sources D and E and your own knowledge of the historical context. [8]

Your answer may include:

Source D:

- *Source D suggests that women had more political freedom. This backs up my own knowledge that 112 women had been elected to the Reichstag by 1932.*
- *Source D says that women entered the workforce. Although this supports my knowledge that women made up 36% of the German workforce, this was equal to female employment in 1918.*
- *Source D also states that women had the freedom to earn their own wage. While this is true, there was still a 33% pay gap between men and women.*
- *This source was a newspaper article intended to be made public. The author was also a woman, so she may have wanted to portray changes in women's lives positively.*
- *This source is just one woman's experience so it may not be representative of how other people saw women at the time.*
- *The source only mentions the positive aspects of the changing position of women and doesn't mention any of the negative changes, so her account is not balanced.*

Source E:

- *This source shows a woman in what appears to be a nightclub drinking alcohol. This supports my own knowledge that some women drank alcohol and enjoyed going to bars.*
- *The woman in the centre is wearing a low-cut dress. This supports my knowledge that women had more freedom over what they wore during the Weimar Republic.*
- *This source was a cartoon from a satirical magazine which was meant to be made public. Satirical magazines often use exaggeration to ridicule people or groups, so this image could be an exaggeration of what women during the Weimar Republic were like.*
- *This is a cartoon, so it is made up and may not have accurately reflected the behaviour of women during the Weimar Republic.*
- *Source E only portrays the freedoms that women had in their leisure time. It doesn't include any information about other freedoms, for example in employment or politics.*

This question should be marked in accordance with the levels-based mark scheme on page 61.

Make sure your answer to this question is in paragraphs and full sentences. Bullet points have been used in this example answer to suggest some information you could include.

CULTURAL CHANGES

Culture thrived in Weimar Germany. Freedom of speech was law, and this allowed freedom of expression to grow.

Culture and the Weimar Republic

The recovery of the economy and a move away from a more traditional way of life inspired cultural changes. Government grants also helped new artistic movements such as 'New Objectivism', 'Modernism' and 'Expressionism' to flourish.

Cinema and entertainment

The 1920s were a golden age for German **cinema**, and directors were often influenced by artistic movements. For example, Fritz Lang's 1927 film 'Metropolis' was heavily influenced by Modernism.

The theatre, cabaret and jazz also became very popular among young people who lived in the cities.

Literature

'All Quiet on the Western Front' was a novel by Erich-Maria Remarque. Published in 1929, it embraced New Realism, and described the horrors of war.

Consequence   Cultural change

Not everyone agreed with these cultural changes. The left-wing felt that money should be spent relieving poverty and poor social conditions. The right-wing were angry at the erosion of traditional values.

Art and architecture

Painter, Otto Dix was a 'New Objectivist' who believed in portraying life as it is. Although he criticised Weimar, his work was popular, as was the work of Georg Grosz, whose famous painting 'Grey Day' showed a society that was not working for everyone.

Walther Gropius led a Modernist design movement called Bauhaus. It used clean, simple lines and influenced design, furniture and architecture.

An example of Bauhaus architecture

HITLER'S EARLY CAREER

In 1919, Adolf Hitler, a veteran of World War I, became an informant on left-wing political meetings.

The German Workers' Party (DAP)

In September 1919, Hitler was asked to report on meetings of the **German Workers' Party** (DAP). The party had been founded in Munich by Anton Drexler in February 1919, and only numbered around 50 members. The DAP was nationalist, and so mostly appealed to right-wing voters, but Drexler had some left-wing, socialist ideas. For example, he wanted to cap the profits of big companies. It was these socialist ideas that Hitler was asked to inform upon.

As an informant, Hitler was ordered to join the party. Once he was a member, he began to take control. He was a skilled speaker, and his speeches were full of enthusiasm. In January 1920, Drexler asked him to oversee recruitment and propaganda.

Hitler began attacking:
- the Treaty of Versailles
- the Weimar Government
- 'November Criminals'
- Jews and Communists through Dolchstoss (see **page 5**)

Adolf Hitler in the early 1920s.

THE TWENTY-FIVE POINT PROGRAMME

In August, the DAP was renamed to include National Socialist (Nationalsozialistische) at the beginning. It became the NSDAP, or the Nazi Party.

Nazi Party ideology

In February 1920, Hitler and Drexler drew up the **Twenty-Five Point Programme**. The Twenty-Five Points were ideas, rather than concrete policies, but they appealed to both left-wing and right-wing voters. They were the basis of Hitler's actions until his death, and included:
- A strong, united Germany
- The Treaty of Versailles should be ignored
- Germany should be governed by a single leader, rather than being a democracy
- The superiority of the **Aryan** race (tall, blonde-haired, blue-eyed white people)
- Jews were inferior
- Germany should be economically self-sufficient
- Jews and communists threatened the stability of Germany
- Germans needed space to expand, **Lebensraum** (living space), by growing territories

THE EARLY GROWTH AND FEATURES OF THE PARTY

Media and membership

In December 1920, the party bought the newspaper 'Volkische Beobachter' (*People's Observer*) which allowed Hitler to publish his views to a wider audience. Hitler's speeches became more theatrical, and his popularity increased.

Membership of the Nazi Party grew quickly. In 1920 there were 2,000 members, and by 1923, there were 20,000 members.

Leadership and organisation

In July 1921, Hitler defeated Drexler to become **Führer** (leader) of the NSDAP. Hitler developed this further into the Führerprinzip, or Leadership Principle, strengthening his authority.

Hitler's closest allies were given key positions, which reinforced his control.

Ruldolf Hess

A WWI veteran who became Hitler's second-in-command. Hess was wealthy and brought money to the Nazi Party.

Ernst Röhm

Röhm was a former army officer who founded the **SA** (see **page 19**).

Julius Streicher

Allowed the Nazi Party to use his newspaper 'Der Sturmer' (*The Stormer*), to give the Nazis an audience outside Bavaria (a region in the south-east of Germany).

Hermann Goering

Goering flew with the German Air Force in WWI. He joined the Nazi Party in 1922 and was given command of the SA in 1923. He became one of the most powerful members of the Nazi Party.

Der Sturmer was an antisemitic newspaper used to spread the Nazi Party's propaganda.

THE ROLE OF THE SA

The SA

In August 1921, **Ernst Röhm** set up The **SA** (**Sturmabteilung**) to become the **Nazi Party's private army**. By 1922, there were 800 members. The SA was largely made up of unemployed ex-soldiers, who were angry at how they had been treated following World War I, the November Criminals, and the Treaty of Versailles. Joining the SA gave ex-soldiers employment, a purpose, and a rallying point for their resentment of the Weimar Government.

The SA were used to protect Nazi meetings and rallies, as well as to intimidate other political groups by breaking up their gatherings. Having its own private army made the Nazi Party seem legitimate and gave the impression that it was disciplined and well organised.

Hitler drew his own bodyguard, the Stosstruppen or Shock Troops, from within the SA.

A poster showing a member of the SA

Source F:

An extract taken from the Twenty-Five Point Programme of the NSDAP.

4. *Only a member of the race can be a citizen. A member of the race can only be one who is of German blood, without consideration of creed. Consequently, no Jew can be a member of the race.*

5. *Those who are not citizens must live in Germany as foreigners and must be subject to the laws of non-citizens.*

9. *All citizens must possess equal rights.*

Give **two** things you can infer from Source F about Hitler's Twenty-Five Point Programme.   [4]

1. ***What I can infer:*** *Hitler didn't think that Jews should be citizens.*[1]

    Details in the source that tell me this: *Point 4 says that only a member of the race could be a citizen, and Jews are not members of the race.*[1]

2. ***What I can infer:*** *Jews would be treated differently to other German citizens.*[1]

    Details in the source that tell me this: *Hitler didn't think Jews were citizens, so they would be 'subject to the laws of non-citizens'.*[1]

THE MUNICH PUTSCH

Hitler was confident that the time was right for the Nazis to seize power. In 1923, he led a revolt in Munich known as the **Munich Putsch**.

Reasons for the Munich Putsch

The Munich Putsch is sometimes known as the Beer Hall Putsch.

Discontent with Weimar

Some German people blamed the Weimar Government for economic and social problems like hyperinflation and the occupation of the Ruhr. Hitler wanted to capitalise on this discontent.

Nazi Party's growing strength

In Bavaria, the popularity of the Nazi Party was rising, and its membership was growing steadily. The SA now numbered in their thousands and provided support on the streets. Hitler thought that he had the support of nationalist politicians in Bavaria, including Seisser, Kahr and Lossow. Seisser was head of the Bavarian State Police, Kahr ran the Bavarian government and Lossow ran the German Army in Bavaria.

Examples abroad

In 1922, Mussolini had taken power in Italy using a private Fascist army in the March on Rome. Hitler thought he could replicate this in Germany.

Events of the Munich Putsch, 1923

October – Hitler conspired with Seisser, Kahr and Lossow to lead a revolt in Munich.

4th November – Seisser, Kahr and Lossow changed their minds and called off the revolt. Hitler had already gathered troops and wasn't prepared to back down.

8th November – Seisser, Kahr and Lossow held a meeting at the Bürgerbräukeller (a beerhall) on the outskirts of Munich. Hitler and 600 SA stormed in, declaring a takeover of the state of Bavaria. At gunpoint, Hitler got the support of Kahr and Lossow. Röhm had taken control of key police and army HQs but hadn't taken the main army barracks.

9th November – At 5am, Seisser, Kahr and Lossow were allowed to leave the Bürgerbräukeller. By late morning, Hitler and 3,000 supporters marched into Munich, expecting to seize power. The marchers were stopped in the centre of town by armed police because Kahr had called in reinforcements. A fight broke out, and 16 Nazis and 4 policemen died. Many more were wounded.

Consequences of the Munich Putsch

11th November – Hitler was captured and arrested.

Hitler was found guilty of treason. He received a five-year prison sentence, and the Nazi Party was banned. While in prison, he wrote **Mein Kampf** (see **page 21**) Hitler only served nine months in prison and the ban was lifted in 1925.

Hitler was able to use his imprisonment in **propaganda**. His trial got a lot of publicity, and it showed that he was a man of action, who was prepared to go to prison for his beliefs.

REASONS FOR LIMITED SUPPORT FOR THE NAZI PARTY, 1924–28

For a while, the Nazi Party had limited support. Hitler realised he needed to get elected to get into power, so he reorganised and relaunched the Nazi Party.

Success of the Weimar Government

The Weimar Government had stabilised German society, partly because Stresemann's policies worked for all classes. The working class would not vote Nazi while there was plenty of work, good pay, and fair conditions. The middle class benefitted from trade developments and the upper class enjoyed seeing Germany restored to the international community.

Hindenburg was President, and the 78-year-old war hero was very popular with voters. This meant fewer supporters for the Nazis, who were seen as a risky option while things were going well.

Mein Kampf

Hitler realised that overthrowing the Weimar Government with violence would not work and set about becoming electable instead. He wrote **Mein Kampf** (*My Struggle*) in prison, which was an autobiographical manifesto that outlined his ideology.

A cartoon from 1924 showing Hitler going to prison.

Mein Kampf key ideas

Jewish conspiracy

Jews were undermining German society by intermarrying, being members of the SPD and working in German industry.

Aryan race

Aryans were non-Jewish Germans who upheld traditional values. Hitler believed they were destined to rule.

Socialism

Land would be redistributed to those who worked on it.

One leader

A Führer would control a **totalitarian state** (a government that has complete control over the lives of its citizens), holding power over everyone and everything.

Nationalism

Hitler wanted to make Germany strong again, by breaking the Treaty of Versailles.

Significance   Mein Kampf

Mein Kampf was published in 1925 (with Volume 2 following a year later). By 1933, it had sold 240,000 copies, and by the end of the war in 1945 about 10 million copies had been sold or distributed in Germany.

Key features of the Nazi Party reorganisation

Hitler was released from prison in 1924 and began reorganising the Nazi Party. He realised that the party needed a strong national structure to attract voters.

- Munich became the 'Capital of the Movement', and departments such as finance, foreign affairs and education were established in Munich in preparation for government.

- Hitler created organisations within the Nazi Party, for example, the **German Students' League** (later called the **Hitler Youth**). This made people feel included and encouraged widespread support across all sections of society.

- **Gauleiters** were created. These men oversaw German regions (Gau) for the Nazis. Hitler used these positions to ensure nationwide Nazi control.

- The Schutzstaffel, or **SS** (Nazi protection squad) was created. The SS were more controlled than the SA. They were carefully selected and became Hitler's personal guard. A leading Nazi Party official called **Himmler** soon rose to take control of the SS.

1926 The Bamberg Conference

The **Bamberg Conference** was a meeting of 60 high-ranking Nazis. Hitler used it to:
- put an end to dissent that was emerging in the northern branches of the party.
- establish his position as the ultimate leader of the Nazi Party.
- promote the Twenty-Five Point Programme as the core ideology of the party.

The conference saw the Party move towards nationalism, and away from socialism.

1923–9 The Lean Years

The period between 1923–29 is known as the Nazi Party's **Lean Years**. Although the party's popularity and membership were growing, it struggled to win seats in the Reichstag. For example, in May 1928, the Nazis only had 12 seats out of a possible 491.

However, by 1929, there were 130,000 members, and things were beginning to change.

A poster from the late 1920s by the German Democratic Party which says, "Clean up the Reich!" showing a German man sweeping away Swastikas and communist red stars.

Interpretation 1:

On the surface the Beer-Hall Putsch seemed to be a failure, but actually it was a brilliant achievement for a political nobody. In a few hours Hitler catapulted his scarcely known, unimportant movement into headlines throughout Germany and the world. Moreover, he learned an important lesson: direct action was not the way to political power. It was necessary that he seek political victory by winning the masses to his side and also by attracting the support of wealthy industrialists. Then he could ease his way to political supremacy by legal means.

Encyclopaedia of the Third Reich, by Louis L Synder

Interpretation 2:

With the failure of the Munich putsch, the worst of the internal crisis was over. The Nazi Party and other organisations of the extreme right were forbidden throughout Germany, as well as the Communist Party. In the crucial test of the autumn weeks of 1923, the Republic had maintained itself against challenges from both right and left.

The Weimar Republic, by Eberhard Kolb

Study Interpretations 1 and 2. They give different views about the significance of the Munich Putsch.

What is the main difference between them? Explain your answer, using details from both interpretations. [4]

A main difference is that Interpretation 1 suggests that the Munich Putsch was a success for Hitler and the Nazi Party[1] because it gave them notoriety and publicity both at home and abroad.[1] On the other hand, Interpretation 2 suggests that the failure of the Munich Putsch was a success for the Weimar Government,[1] because it was able to put down the uprising, and use the revolt as a reason to ban extreme political groups, such as the Nazi Party and the Communist Party.[1]

THE GROWTH OF UNEMPLOYMENT

The Wall Street Crash

Stresemann died in 1929, and three weeks later, on 24th October 1929, the US stock market dived. This was known as the **Wall Street Crash**, and it sparked financial panic across the globe. Shares were sold at huge losses as people tried to regain some of the money they had invested. Within a week, about $4000 million was lost as prices tumbled further.

In Germany, the banks collapsed. The USA recalled its loans from the Dawes Plan (see **page 10**), and ordinary people, remembering hyperinflation, withdrew cash from the banks. German industry was devastated by loans being recalled. Confidence plummeted and economic collapse followed. Prior to the Wall Street Crash, unemployment was 1.25 million. By 1932 this had risen to 5.1 million.

By January 1933:
- 40% factory workers had lost their jobs
- 50% of 16–30-year-olds were out of work
- 60% university graduates were unemployed

Even those in work suffered pay cuts. Meanwhile, the government could not afford to pay benefits, so had to raise taxes. Exports fell by 50% as iron and steel production fell dramatically and homelessness rose. The period following the Wall Street Crash is known as the **Great Depression**.

The failure of the Weimar Government

In March 1930, Heinrich Brüning was appointed as Chancellor to help deal with the situation. His strategies of raising taxes and cutting benefits earned him the name the 'Hunger Chancellor'.

Brüning's policies gained little support in the Reichstag, so he had to use Article 48 (see **page 3**) of the Weimar Constitution to pass laws. President Hindenburg had issued five in 1930, but by 1932, this had risen to 66. The government seemed to be acting as if Germany were no longer a democracy and ruling by decrees. The German people began to look to other political groups for solutions to the economic crisis.

Here are some examples of Nazi election posters from the early 1930s showing how they tried to appeal to working-class voters.

Left: 'Workers who work with the head or the fist choose the frontline soldier, Hitler!'.

Right: 'Those against corruption vote for the National Socialist Hitler Movement!'

Growth in support of the Communist party

Large numbers of Germans began to vote for the extreme left and right, Communists (KPD) and Nazis (NSDAP), in the hope that these parties could solve the country's problems.

The KPD's share of the votes rose by almost 50% from 1928 to 1932, making them the biggest Communist party outside the USSR. The KPD was a popular choice among the working-classes, as they claimed communism was the way out of poverty and hardship.

Growth in support for the Nazi Party

By 1932 Hitler felt he had enough support to challenge Hindenburg for the Presidency. He lost, but won 13 million votes, showing his increasing political reputation.

1932 Presidential election

Hindenburg	Independent	53%	
Hitler	Nazi Party	36%	
Thälmann	KPD	10%	

Source G: A Nazi campaign poster from 1932 which reads: 'Our last hope: Hitler'.

Give **two** things you can infer from Source G about the political situation in Germany in 1932. [4]

1. *What I can infer:* The Nazi Party didn't support the Weimar Government.[1]

    Details in the source that tell me this: Hitler is described as Germany's 'last hope' which suggests that the Nazi Party didn't believe the Weimar Government was going to help people.[1]

2. *What I can infer:* The Great Depression was an opportunity for Hitler to gain support.[1]

    Details in the source that tell me this: Promising 'hope' would have appealed to Germans suffering unemployment and poverty during the Great Depression.[1]

REASONS FOR THE GROWTH IN SUPPORT FOR THE NAZI PARTY

The German people were desperate for solutions to the problems of the Great Depression, and they had lost faith in the Weimar Government.

The appeal of Hitler and the Nazis

The Nazi Party's popularity soared in during the Great Depression because it appealed to all members of society.

Upper class

The upper classes usually voted Nationalist and saw the communist KPD as a threat to their livelihood.

Hugenberg, a nationalist businessman and politician, gave Hitler access to nationalist media. **Goebbels**, a Nazi politician and head of propaganda, was able to publish pro-Nazi material in 120 newspapers. The Nazis gained considerable financial support from industrial giants like Thyssen and Krupp.

Working class

Working-class voters were usually a stronghold for the Left, and many moved towards the KPD. Although the Nazi Party didn't gain as much working-class support, Nazi slogans embracing socialist ideals such as 'Work & Bread' won some voters, as did a promise to tackle unemployment. Some did not trust the KPD, and felt the SA (**Sturmabteilung**) brought order to the streets.

Middle class

Middle classes usually voted for moderate parties and feared the KPD.

They were particularly badly hit by the Great Depression. Many liked Hitler's traditional values, especially after the 'moral decline' seen during Weimar. In 1930, they represented two-thirds of the Nazi Party members.

Women

Many women agreed with Nazi messages about traditional values and the importance of homemaking.

Youth

Young people were attracted to the activities of the Nazi Party. **Rallies** (see **page 39**) were exciting and gave young people a feeling of importance.

The SA (Sturmabteilung)

Membership of the SA rose in 1931 from 100,000 to 170,000. The SA outnumbered the KPD's Red Front by a ratio of 3:1.

The SA broke up KPD meetings and rallies, and damaged property, like printing presses. Nazi press reported any fights which broke out between the two groups as the KPD's fault. Judges would often jail KPD members for disorder but would be more lenient towards the SA.

Hitler's appeal and use of propaganda

Hitler's charisma and strong, consistent message offered hope. He played on fears of communism and offered the Jews as scapegoats for society's problems. He also used propaganda to target specific groups to make them feel included and supported. During the 1932 election campaign, he travelled around the country by air, and he made use of radio broadcasts. In July 1932, the Nazis became the largest party in the Reichstag with 230 seats.

Explain why support for the Nazis grew in 1929–32.

You may use the following in your answer:

- the role of Hitler
- the role of the SA

You must also use information of your own. [12]

Your answer may include:

The role of Hitler:
- *Hitler's message and tactics had broad appeal. For example, many women supported his belief in traditional values, and many young people were excited by Nazi rallies.*
- *He used newspapers, radio broadcasts and rallies to spread his message across Germany, and he was a charismatic and inspiring public speaker.*
- *Hitler had reorganised and strengthened the Nazi Party prior to 1929, so when voters were looking for a solution to the Great Depression, the Nazi Party seemed like a viable option.*

The role of the SA:
- *The KPD saw a growth in popularity following the Wall Street Crash, but the SA were used to limit the KPD's influence. The SA disrupted KPD meetings and rallies and damaged their printing presses to stop them spreading their message.*
- *Some working-class Germans felt that the SA brought order to the streets.*

Fear of communism:
- *Many upper- and middle-class Germans saw communism as a threat to their way of life. The Nazi Party offered an alternative.*
- *Large German firms like Krupp and Thyssen also feared communism, so they gave financial support to the Nazi Party. This gave the party more resources and credibility.*

The Wall Street Crash and the Great Depression:
- *Prior to the Wall Street Crash, most Germans were satisfied with the Weimar Government, as there had been stability, job security and improvements to quality of life.*
- *Germans blamed the Weimar Government for the Great Depression which caused many Germans to look to more extreme political parties for solutions.*

The failure of the Weimar Government:
- *Brüning's severe economic policies, such as benefit cuts, were unpopular and people called him the "Hunger Chancellor". The Weimar Government lost support as voters turned elsewhere.*

This question should be marked in accordance with the levels-based mark scheme on page 60.

Make sure your answer to this question is in paragraphs and full sentences. Bullet points have been used in this example answer to suggest some information you could include.

To get top marks, you need to include information other than the bullet points in the question.

HOW HITLER BECAME CHANCELLOR, 1932–33

Political uncertainty and in-fighting helped Hitler become Chancellor in 1932.

A Nazi poster from the election of 1932. An Aryan farmer is shown removing a Jewish businessman and a communist with a pitchfork.

March 1932

President Hindenburg stood for re-election. He did not get the 50% of votes he needed. Hitler and Ernst Thalmann (leader of the KPD) also stood, splitting the vote.

April

Hindenburg won 53% of the vote in a re-run and was re-elected, but Hitler was close behind with 36%.

Brüning (the German Chancellor) banned the SA and SS due to the violence on the streets. He also planned to buy land from rich landowners to house the unemployed. However, there was so much opposition to Brüning that he was forced to resign.

May

Von Papen was selected as Chancellor. He called for elections in July.

Von Papen, and other wealthy ministers, became known as the **Cabinet of Barons**. This group thought they could bring the Nazis into government and use their support, but still control them.

July

The election campaign was violent and up to 100 people died. The Nazis emerged as the largest party, with 230 seats and 37% of the vote (up from 18% in 1930). Hitler had a strong negotiating position.

January 1933

Hitler was sworn in as Chancellor. Although he had power, Hitler was still limited by:

- the Constitution – the Nazis did not have the majority they needed
- the President – Hindenburg despised Hitler
- a mixed Cabinet – only two other Nazis, Frick and Goering, were in the Cabinet.

December

Von Papen was replaced by von Schleicher, who wanted to suspend the Constitution and be given special powers to govern Germany. The President refused. Von Schleicher began plotting a putsch. Von Papen warned Hindenburg of von Schleicher's coup, and proposed Hitler as Chancellor, with himself serving as Vice-Chancellor to control Hitler. Hindenburg reluctantly agreed.

November

Chancellor von Papen called another election. The Nazis were still the largest party but were down to 196 seats. Von Papen resigned.

Source H: Hitler waving from the Chancellery on becoming Chancellor of Germany, 30th January 1933

Source I:

'Papen himself was Vice-Chancellor... and Hindenburg had promised him that he would not receive the Chancellor [Hitler] except in the company of the Vice-Chancellor. This... would enable him to put a brake on the radical Nazi leader. But even more: this government was Papen's conception, his creation, and he was confident that with the help of the staunch old President... he would dominate it.'

The Rise and Fall of the Third Reich, 1960. By William L. Shirer, an American journalist who was in Berlin in 1932–33, for the *Chicago Tribune*.

Study Sources H and I.

How useful are Sources H and I for an enquiry into Hitler's appointment as Chancellor in 1933?

Explain your answer, using Sources H and I and your knowledge of the historical context. [8]

Source H:

- *Source H suggests that Hitler was very popular, as there are huge crowds visible as he is appointed Chancellor. This agrees with my knowledge that Hitler's popularity soared during the Great Depression, and the support he attracted across many sections of society helped the Nazi Party become the largest party in July 1932.*

- *Source H is limited because there is no photographer's name, and it could have been staged for propaganda purposes. We don't know what the photographer has left out of the shot.*

Source I:

- *Source I implies that Hindenburg disliked Hitler and would not see him unless he was with von Papen. This agrees with my knowledge that Hindenburg was very mistrustful of Hitler and was reluctant to appoint him as Chancellor.*

- *Source I is also useful for this enquiry because it suggests that von Papen was arrogant enough to believe he could control Hitler. He expected to be able to "put a brake on" Hitler and 'dominate' the government.*

- *Source I is also useful because of its provenance. Shirer was a journalist in Berlin in 1932–33. He reported for a mainstream American audience, so would have been more objective.*

- *Source I is limited because we don't know how close the author was to the members of the Weimar Government, and he may have relied on second-hand information.*

- *It is also limited by being written with hindsight, so may not be completely accurate.*

This question should be marked in accordance with the levels-based mark scheme on page 61.

Make sure your answer to this question is in paragraphs and full sentences. Bullet points have been used in this example answer to suggest some information you could include.

THE REICHSTAG FIRE

In 1933, Hitler was appointed Chancellor of a democracy. By autumn 1934, he was dictator of a totalitarian regime.

1933 Elections

Elections were scheduled for March 1933. Hitler needed to increase the Nazi Party's seats in the Reichstag so that they had a majority. This would allow him to make changes to the Constitution. In the run up to the elections, Hitler continued to use the SA to disrupt his political opponents.

The Reichstag Fire

On 27th February 1933, the Reichstag building was destroyed by fire. A young Dutch Communist, Marinus van der Lubbe, was accused of starting the fire, and was tried and executed for arson. The fire gave Hitler an advantage.

- The fire caused an increase in anti-communist feeling, and the Nazis encouraged this in their propaganda, including publishing anti-communist conspiracy theories in Nazi-run newspapers.

- President Hindenburg allowed Hitler emergency powers to deal with the Communist threat. Communists were expelled from Parliament and 4,000 more were arrested. This prevented the communists from campaigning prior to the elections on 5th March.

- Fearful of communism, wealthy businessmen such as Krupp, poured millions into the Nazi campaign.

In the March 1933 elections, the Nazis won 44% of the vote, and 288 seats in the Reichstag. The Communists only got 12%, and 81 seats. Hitler used emergency powers to ban them from taking their seats.

The Nazis now had a majority (as the German National People's Party, DNVP, supported the Nazis). However, they were still short of the two-thirds majority they needed to change the Constitution.

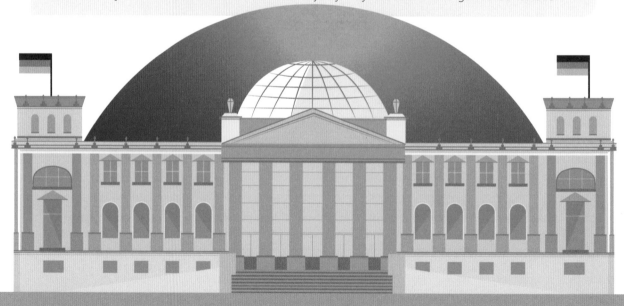

THE ENABLING ACT AND BANNING OF OTHER PARTIES AND TRADE UNIONS

Hitler proposed the Enabling Act to the newly elected Reichstag in March 1933. It allowed Hitler to pass laws without consulting the Reichstag.

As the Reichstag took a vote on the Enabling Act, the SS were stationed inside the chamber, and the SA were outside chanting aggressively. The Enabling Act passed on 23rd March by 444 votes to 94.

The banning of opposition

The Enabling Act allowed Hitler to make laws and sign treaties with foreign powers without the approval of the Reichstag. He used it to wipe out political opposition as well as grassroot opponents.

Political parties

On 14th July, the **Law Against the Formation of Parties** was passed. This meant that no party was legal other than the Nazis. Many simply dissolved themselves rather than be imprisoned.

In elections held in December 1933, the Nazis gained more than 90% of the vote.

Local government

The German federal system meant significant power rested in the hands of the local government officials of the 18 regions. In January 1934, their federal governments were abolished and replaced by Hitler's own appointments.

Trade unions

In May 1933, **trade unions** were banned, and strikes were made illegal. Leaders and officials were arrested. Hitler felt threatened by trade unions because they had the support of the working class.

A new **German Labour Front** (DAF) was created to control workers' rights. If you didn't have a workbook from the DAF, you were unemployed. The DAF was run by a leading Nazi, **Robert Ley**.

The Enabling Act

Proportional Representation in the Weimar Government meant it was sometimes difficult for political parties to reach an agreement. Politicians hoped that the Enabling Act would mean that decisions could be made more quickly.

THE THREAT FROM RÖHM AND THE SA, AND THE NIGHT OF THE LONG KNIVES

By 1933, the SA had around three million members, and Hitler felt threatened by their loyalty to Röhm

The SA and Röhm

The SA, led by Röhm, had been vital in getting Hitler into power, but by 1934, Hitler wanted to get rid of them.

Around 60% of the SA were working-class men who supported socialist policies. Hitler felt that their left-wing ideas could damage his reputation with middle- and upper-class voters.

Germany's army was still limited to 100,000 under the terms of The Treaty of Versailles. Hitler, and army generals, feared that Röhm wanted to bring the army under his control within the SA. Hitler didn't want to anger the German military.

Himmler and Goering resented the power that Röhm had. The SS were nominally under Röhm, and Himmler wanted more independence and power. His 52,000 men were no match for Röhm's SA. Goering's Gestapo (secret police) also came under Röhm, and Goering wanted to rise above Röhm.

Hitler was worried about Röhm's loyalty. The SS warned Hitler of a plot being hatched by Röhm.

The Night of the Long Knives

On 30th June 1934, **The Night of the Long Knives** took place. Hitler called together 100 top SA leaders. The SS arrested them. Overnight, Röhm and others were murdered.

Hitler took the opportunity to remove threats beyond the SA. Von Schleicher (see **page 28**), Gregor Strasser (one of Hitler's oldest allies) and von Kahr (who had turned against him during the Munich Putsch) were among the victims.

Von Papen was luckier. As Vice-Chancellor, his murder might have been too much for Hindenburg to take, but von Papen's staff were shot or arrested.

These actions were illegal, so Hitler passed a law on 3rd July making them legal using the Enabling Act.

Aftermath of the Night of the Long Knives

Hitler justified his actions by claiming that the victims had been plotting to overthrow the government. Hitler maintained he did what was necessary to protect Germany.

Goebbels used the Night of the Long Knives as propaganda. Nazi-controlled media promoted the strength of the Führer and the police agencies and painted those murdered as traitors and criminals.

HITLER BECOMES FÜHRER

When President Hindenburg died in 1934, Hitler immediately declared himself Führer. He had been using that title, but only as leader of the Nazi Party. Now, he combined the roles of Chancellor and President: **Der Führer** of Germany.

Hitler insisted the Army take an oath of allegiance to him as their Commander-in-Chief. Finally, on 19th August, a Plebiscite (people's vote) was held. 90% voted to confirm Hitler as Germany's Führer. This marked the end of the Weimar Republic.

Explain why Hitler was able to become Der Führer of Germany in the years 1933–1934.

You may use the following in your answer:

- the Reichstag Fire
- the Enabling Act

You must also use information of your own. [12]

Your answer may include:

The Reichstag Fire:

- *A communist was blamed for starting the Reichstag Fire, so Hitler was able to use this to suppress communist opposition in the lead up to the elections. Communist politicians were expelled from the Reichstag, and 4,000 communists were imprisoned.*
- *The fire saw a rise in anti-communist feeling, and the Nazis were able to capitalise on that with their propaganda.*
- *Wealthy business owners who were fearful of communism gave millions to the Nazi Party ahead of their election campaign.*

The Enabling Act:

- *The act meant that the Chancellor, Hitler, could propose new laws and that these new laws could override the Weimar Constitution. This effectively gave Hitler the ability to pass his own laws and gave him the power of a dictator.*
- *Hitler used the Enabling Act to pass the Law Against the Formation of Parties. This banned all other political parties in Germany and meant that the Nazi Party was the only political party. Elections held at the end of 1933 saw the Nazi Party win over 90% of the vote.*
- *Hitler also used the Enabling Act to suppress grassroot opposition. He passed a law banning trade unions and strikes.*

Other information:

- *Röhm and the SA had considerable power and were a threat to Hitler. Hitler had Röhm and hundreds of SA members murdered during the Night of the Long Knives to prevent them from challenging his authority. Hitler used the Enabling Act to legalise his actions and painted the victims as criminals in pro-Nazi propaganda.*
- *The death of President Hindenburg in 1934 allowed Hitler to become both President and Chancellor of Germany, and he declared himself Der Führer.*

This question should be marked in accordance with the levels-based mark scheme on page 60.

Make sure your answer to this question is in paragraphs and full sentences. Bullet points have been used in this example answer to suggest some information you could include.

To get top marks, you need to include information other than the bullet points in the question.

THE ROLE OF THE GESTAPO, SS AND SD

The totalitarian state needed control of all elements of police and secret police. By 1936, Heinrich Himmler and the SS oversaw every aspect of policing.

Nazi Police

Hitler used the power given to him by the **Enabling Act**. Officials were allowed to read people's letters, listen to their phone calls and search their homes. German police forces were also used to ensure conformity and loyalty to Hitler.

The SS

The black-shirted Nazi elite worked without fear of the law. They were fiercely loyal to both Himmler and Hitler. The SS were expected to uphold the notion of the mythical Aryan race. They had to be extremely fit, and recruits had to marry to promote racial purity. Homosexuals in the SS were rooted out mercilessly.

Following the Night of the Long Knives the SA was weakened, and had less involvement in maintaining the Nazi police state.

The SD (Sicherheitsdienst)

A uniformed police force who spied on and monitored the activities of known opposition. Details were logged and kept in the 'Brown House', the party HQ in Munich.

The Gestapo

The Secret State Police. They looked for potential criticism of the State, Party or Führer. They used phone tapping and informants. Once arrested, a person would be prosecuted without trial. The **Gestapo** were the only group allowed to send prisoners to concentration camps.

There were about 30,000 Gestapo officers. In 1939, they had arrested 160,000 opponents for political offences. 80% of those arrested were not uncovered by the Gestapo, they were turned in by the public. The Nazis used fear to control the public.

The Creation of the Police State

Himmler's grasp of the police state grew stronger over time, and he was central to Hitler's control. Heydrich was Himmler's choice as administrator. Between them, they ensured Hitler's totalitarian ideals were carried out.

1929 Himmler took command of Hitler's 'protection' using the SS.

1931 Himmler set up SD, and Heydrich was appointed leader of SD.

1933 Gestapo were set up by Goering. Concentration camps began at Dachau.

1934 SS had 52,000 members. Gestapo were placed under SS.

1936 The Gestapo were placed under Heydrich, by Himmler.

1939 The SS had 240,000 members.

CONCENTRATION CAMPS AND NAZI CONTROL OF THE LEGAL SYSTEM

Concentration camps

The first **concentration camp** was set up at Dachau, outside Munich, in March 1933. The first prisoners were opposition politicians and trade unionists. In October 1933, the first women's camp was established at Moringen.

By 1939, there were six camps, away from the public gaze. Inmates suffered brutal conditions, hard labour, and 're-education'. Many prisoners never left.

Nazi control of Judges

In October 1933, the **National Socialist League for the Maintenance of Law** was established by Hitler. All judges had to be members, and each of its 10,000 members could be banned from working if they were removed from the League. Judges were expected to make rulings that favoured the Nazi Party.

People's Court

In 1934, the **People's Court** was set up. It was a court with no jury, so the judge made decisions. Sessions were held in secret and dealt with treason and other serious political crimes. There was no right of appeal. By 1939, the People's Court had sentenced 534 people to death. Hitler would check on sentences and punishments.

Interpretation 3:

The Nazi world was an empire of total force, with no restraints. It was a world composed of masters and slaves, in which gentleness, kindness, pity, the respect for law, and a taste for freedom were no longer virtues, but unforgivable crimes. It was a world in which one could only obey by crawling and killing on orders... It was a world where people exterminated for pleasure and the murderers were treated as heroes.

Jacques Delarue, *The Gestapo: A History of Horror*

Interpretation 4:

Nazism seemed to many just an extreme version of what [most Germans] had always believed in or taken for granted. It was nationalistic, respectful of the armed forces, socially conservative, opposed to laziness, hostile to eccentric or incomprehensive ideas that came from cities... and avid to achieve 'greatness' for Germany. They welcomed parts of Nazi political and social views and told themselves that the rest was less important or was not meant seriously.

Walter Rinderle and Bernard Norling, *The Nazi Impact on a German Village*

1. Study Interpretations 3 and 4. They give different views about Nazi control of the German population in the years 1933–39.

   What is the main difference between the views? Explain your answer, using details from both interpretations. [4]

   A main difference is that Interpretation 3 suggests that the German population was forced to obey the Nazi Party.[1] It states that Nazi Germany was a world of 'masters and slaves'.[1] However, Interpretation 4 suggests that the German public supported the Nazi Party willingly,[1] because they believed and agreed with Nazi policies.[1]

Source J: Gestapo officers recording prisoners at a concentration camp

Source K: Crowds at a Nazi parade, 1935

2. Suggest **one** reason why Interpretations 3 and 4 give different views about the control of the German population in the years 1933–1939. You may use Sources J and K to help you. [4]

   The Interpretations may differ because the authors have chosen to focus on different details. Interpretation 3 focuses on Nazi methods of control,[1] such as the Gestapo and concentration camps shown in Source J.[1] Whereas Interpretation 4 focuses on German support for Nazi policies, such as respect for the German military.[1] This is reinforced by Source K which shows crowds saluting German soldiers.[1]

NAZI POLICIES TOWARDS THE CATHOLIC AND PROTESTANT CHURCHES

Most of the German population were Christian – either Catholic or Protestant. Christian beliefs were at odds with Nazi ideology.

Hitler and the Church

Hitler believed that the Church should follow and encourage Nazi policies and ideology. The Church had a lot of influence over the German population, and Hitler wanted to control the Church, and use it to promote Nazi ideas.

The Concordat

In July 1933, the Catholic Church signed a **Concordat** (agreement) with Hitler which agreed:

- Freedom of worship and education in faith schools.
- Priests would not take part in politics.
- Bishops to swear loyalty to the regime.

The Concordat reassured some that Hitler was attempting to improve relations with the Catholic community.

However, Hitler did not take long to break the agreement. By the end of 1933, some priests had been arrested and some sent to concentration camps. By 1939, Catholic schools had either fallen into line, or had been forced to close. Monasteries were shut and the Catholic Youth League was banned.

In 1937, the Pope (the head of the Catholic Church) condemned Hitler's actions in a letter to Catholic Churches in Germany. However, many Catholics were too afraid to speak out against Hitler.

The Protestant Reich Church

The Protestant Church represented about two-thirds of the German population. In 1933, Hitler made Ludwig Müller, a Nazi supporter, the Reich Bishop of Germany. By 1936, those pastors who supported the Nazi regime had set up the **Reich Church**.

- Some Protestant churches used the swastika instead of the cross.
- The Old Testament (the portion used by Jews) was removed from teaching.
- Some churches replaced the Bible with Mein Kampf.
- Jews were not to be baptised into the Reich Church.

Protestant churches felt pressurised to support the Nazi Party, but they were never fully under Hitler's control.

GOEBBELS AND THE MINISTRY OF PROPAGANDA

The Nazi Party controlled politics, religion, and the justice system, but it also wanted to control what people thought and felt.

Goebbels and the Ministry of Propaganda

Propaganda is a way of making people believe certain information to win their support. Joseph Goebbels oversaw Nazi propaganda from 1930, and he created the **Ministry of Public Enlightenment and Propaganda** in 1933. The ministry had various departments, including music, film, literature, and radio, which ensured that Nazi messages appeared in every walk of life, including sport, culture, and the arts.

Nazi messages

Propaganda repeated Nazi ideology, for example, blaming Jews and communists for Germany's problems, rejecting the Treaty of Versailles, and highlighting the importance of traditional values.

Nazi propaganda often targeted specific groups. For example, this election poster from 1931 promises "Work, freedom and bread". This slogan would have appealed to working-class voters concerned with poverty and unemployment following the Great Depression.

Nazi propaganda also reinforced the 'cult of the Führer', which portrayed Hitler as a god-like saviour of Germany. The Nazi greeting of "Heil Hitler" (hail Hitler) emphasised the importance of Hitler, and slogans such as 'one people, one empire, one leader' reminded people of their loyalty to him.

The **swastika** (the Nazi symbol adopted by Hitler) was everywhere. It featured on government uniforms, public buildings, and posters.

Significance   Effect of propaganda

There is some disagreement about the effectiveness of Nazi propaganda. Some people believe that rather than influencing people's opinions, propaganda just reinforced beliefs that already existed. For example, the stab-in-the-back theories (**page 5**) show that there were already widespread antisemitic feelings and a hatred of the Treaty of Versailles prior to the Nazi party. Whether propaganda changed people's minds or just reinforced their beliefs, it was an important reason for Nazi support.

Nazi use of media and censorship

Goebbels ensured that the ideas and views of anyone opposed to the Nazis were censored. He wanted to prevent Germans from seeing or hearing anything that could be considered anti-Nazi.

Press

- The **Editors Law** of 1933 banned left-wing and Jewish journalists.
- The German Press Agency controlled which foreign news stories were published.
- If a newspaper failed to report on Goebbels' press briefing, it could be shut down.
- In 1935 alone, over 1600 newspapers were closed.

Radio

- 70% of homes had a radio by 1939.
- All radio stations were under Nazi control.
- Broadcasts were often made by leading Nazis.
- No foreign stations were picked up.
- There were huge speakers in factories, streets, and stadiums.

Rallies

The Nazis had held rallies since the 1920s. Once in power, they made them even grander to showcase Nazi power and control. Thousands of people would attend the rallies to hear speeches from Hitler and other leading Nazis and watch soldiers march in formation. Nuremberg was the 'City of the Party Rallies', and the 1934 rally was made into a propaganda film, *Triumph of the Will*, by Nazi filmmaker, Leni Riefenstahl.

Sport

Sporting events were an ideal propaganda opportunity to promote Nazism to vast crowds. Visiting teams often had to pay respect, for example the England football squad performed a Nazi salute prior to a game against Germany in 1938. This gave Nazism international recognition. Sporting victories also promoted the Nazi ideals of strong, healthy citizens.

1936   Berlin Olympics

The **Olympics** were held in Berlin in 1936. This was an important propaganda opportunity for Goebbels.
- There was a full stadium with 110,000 people cheering and waving banners.
- Germany topped the medal table with 33 Golds.
- The event was well organised to show Nazi efficiency.
- Leni Riefenstahl captured exciting footage.
- **But:** Jesse Owens, an African American athlete, won four gold medals. This undermined the Nazi idea of the superiority of the Aryan race.

Censorship

- Press releases about the Olympics and letters sent by foreign teams were censored.

  This was to ensure that negative stories about Germany didn't leak to the rest of the world.

NAZI CONTROL OF CULTURE

Nazism promoted traditional values, such as family, nature, discipline and self-sacrifice, and these were reoccurring themes in culture.

Nazi control of the arts

From 1933, Goebbels controlled the new **Reich Chamber of Culture**. He could ban anything that wasn't consistent with Nazism.

Art

The Reich Chamber of Visual Arts was set up under Goebbels in 1933. It aimed to promote and encourage Aryan art. Artists had to apply and needed an Aryan certificate to be accepted and 42,000 artists joined. Non-members' works were confiscated, and non-members could not make money by teaching. In 1936 alone, 12,000 artworks were removed from museums and taken from private collections, among them works by Picasso and Van Gogh.

In 1937, German artists were invited to participate in the Great German Art Exhibition. Only art that had been approved by the Nazi Government was put on display. Approved artworks showed Germany's greatness, military strength, or the Aryan race.

Architecture

Albert Speer was the leading Nazi architect. He was commissioned to redesign the Reich Chancellery and the parade ground at Nuremberg. Nazi buildings were grand and imposing and were often influenced by Roman and Greek styles to reflect the glory of their empires.

Music

Jazz was banned. The Nazis felt it was too closely linked to the 'degenerate' days of Weimar, and it was also associated with 'inferior' Black musicians. Jewish German composers, like Mendelssohn, were also banned. Hitler's favourite composer – Wagner – was widely performed. Beethoven, Bach, and traditional German folk music were all acceptable.

Theatre

Cheaply produced, propaganda-filled plays were staged. Any plays by Jewish or left-wing playwrights were banned, but classics by authors such as Shakespeare were allowed.

Film

Cinema was very popular. In 1933, audiences in Germany reached 250 million.

Films were used to reinforce Nazi ideology, for example, *The Eternal Jew* was an antisemitic film which compared Jews to rats which spread diseases. The film was produced at a time when leading Nazis didn't think their persecution of Jews had enough support amongst the German population.

In every cinema, a newsreel full of propaganda messages was shown for 45 minutes before each film.

Literature

Books by Jewish and left-wing authors were not only banned, but they were burned in great piles. Thousands of authors fled abroad, including Brecht, Mann and the scientist, Einstein.

Source L:

But the most brilliant propagandist technique will yield no success unless one fundamental principle is borne in mind constantly and with unflagging attention. It must confine itself to a few points and repeat them over and over. Here, as so often in this world, persistence is the first and most important requirement for success.

Adolf Hitler, *Mein Kampf*, 1925

Source M: Goebbels speaking at a Nazi rally in 1938

How useful are Sources L and M for an enquiry into Nazi use of propaganda?

Explain your answer, using Sources L and M and your own knowledge of the historical context. [8]

Source L:

- *Source L suggests that Hitler thought successful propaganda repeated the same information over and over. This agrees with my own knowledge that the Nazi Party repeated simple, effective messages on their propaganda for example, 'one people, one empire, one leader' which reinforced Nazi ideology of German unity under Hitler's leadership.*

- *As well as repeating slogans, Nazi propaganda put the swastika everywhere, including uniforms, hanging from buildings, and emblazoned on posters.*

- *Source L is useful because it was written by Hitler himself. Mein Kampf was also an important piece of propaganda for the Nazis as it helped to spread Nazi ideology, and over 10 million copies had been distributed by the end of 1945.*

- *The source may be limited in its usefulness because it was written before Hitler became Der Führer, so his opinions may have changed after he came to power.*

Source M:

- *Source M is useful because it shows Goebbels addressing the Nazi Party at a rally. As the Minister for Propaganda, Goebbels would have used rallies to spread Nazi messages.*

- *Rallies were used as a propaganda tool to display the power of the Nazi Party. This photo supports my own knowledge that rallies featured impressive displays of Nazi soldiers, speeches by leading Nazi members and flags with the swastika.*

- *Rallies weren't the only form of Nazi propaganda. They also used radio broadcasts, posters, literature, and theatres. This source is limited in its usefulness for enquiries about other types of Nazi propaganda.*

- *Although most Nazi rallies in the 1930s were attended by thousands of people, we cannot see the size of the crowd that Goebbels is addressing, or what else is outside the shot.*

- *We do not know who took the photo, and if the photo was taken to be published. The photo could have been staged and may not be genuine.*

This question should be marked in accordance with the levels-based mark scheme on page 61.

Make sure your answer to this question is in paragraphs and full sentences. Bullet points have been used in this example answer to suggest some information you could include.

THE EXTENT OF SUPPORT FOR THE NAZI REGIME

Germans had voted for Hitler in large numbers and many approved of his leadership.

The Nazis had a lot of support...	... but it was difficult to speak out
• Nazi policies had restored the economy and created employment opportunities.	• The Enabling Act banned other political parties. There was no alternative to the Nazis.
• Hitler promised to tear up the hated Treaty of Versailles.	• The Gestapo sought out and punished opposition.
• Under Hitler, Germany was once again a proud nation.	• Censorship made sure that anti-Nazi views could not be spread.
• Hitler brought stability and aimed to stop the spread of communism.	• Nazi totalitarianism controlled churches, trade unions, education, youth movements and local government. There was no easy way to show opposition.

OPPOSITION FROM THE CHURCHES

In 1933, Protestants set up the **Pastors' Emergency League** (**PEL**). In 1934, the PEL founded the **Confessing Church**. The Confessing Church opposed the introduction of the **Reich Church**, and over 6000 pastors joined.

The Reich Church (25% of churches)	The Confessing Church (75% of churches)
Central control by Nazis	Localised control
State interference in services	Allowed no interference
Jews banned from converting to Christianity	Jews allowed to convert
No teaching of the Old Testament	Old Testament taught

The Nazi response to the Confessing Church was to arrest members of the PEL. Over 800 pastors were sent to concentration camps, among them was **Pastor Martin Niemöller**.

In 1924 and 1933, he voted Nazi and supported Hitler as Chancellor. However, Niemöller resented Nazi interference in the Church, and he opposed the regime from 1934, so his phone was tapped by the Gestapo. He was arrested several times, but in 1937 he was sent to a concentration camp. He was liberated from the camp in 1945.

The Catholic Church took its spiritual lead from the Pope. The Concordat (**see page 37)** meant many Catholic priests conformed to Nazi controls, at least until 1937. Some opposed the regime, especially after the Pope spoke out, and around 400 were sent to the Dachau concentration camp.

OPPOSITION FROM THE YOUNG

Most young people conformed to the Nazi regime by joining Nazi youth groups and attending rallies. However, there was some opposition to the Nazi Party amongst the young.

Swing Youth

The **Swing Youth** (or Swing Kids) rebelled against Nazi censorship of American music and fashion. Its members were mostly young people who lived in cities. The movement started in Hamburg and spread through northern cities such as Kiel and Berlin. The Swing Youth resisted some aspects of the regime, but there was very little open opposition.

Edelweiss Pirates

Mostly city-based, they were working-class young people who wore the white edelweiss flower to show their association with other 'pirates'. The boys hated the idea of forced military service, so in defiance of Nazi values, they grew their hair long and wore American fashions. For the most part, **Edelweiss Pirates** resisted the conformity of joining the Hitler Youth groups.

These youth resistance groups were not organised for political change. Instead, they wanted to protest restrictions on their lives. Their opposition to the Nazi Party was limited, and membership was small, approximately 10,000 compared with the eight million members of the Hitler Youth in 1939.

NAZI POLICIES TOWARDS WOMEN

The Nazi Party expected women to uphold traditional values, and to be obedient wives and homemakers.

Nazi views on women

According to the Nazi Party, the ideal German woman looked and behaved a certain way.

Desirable	Undesirable
Natural looking, Aryan	Wearing make-up, non-Aryan
Hair neat and tied back	Hair too long or free-flowing
Married with children	Single
Traditional, modest dress	Modern, immodest dress
Homemaker	Living with parents or friends
Not working	Employed

Nazi policies strengthened control over women's lives

Women were equal to men, but had a different role as wives, mothers, and protectors of the Aryan race. Nazi women were expected to follow the three Ks – **Kinder**, **Küche**, **Kirche** (children, kitchen, church).

Between 1930–33, the birth rate fell in Germany. The Nazi Party introduced new policies to try to reverse this. They wanted to increase the German population to provide the soldiers and workers of the future. By 1936, there were 480,000 more births than deaths.

1933	The **Law for the Encouragement of Marriage** paid a wife up to 1000 Marks as a loan, but only if she stopped paid work. Each child born would see 25% of the loan written off. Women were discouraged from jobs such as teacher, doctor or civil servant. The **Sterilisation Law** allowed Jewish women to have an abortion, but non-Jews could not.
1934	360,000 women had given up work because of Nazi encouragement. All women's clubs and organisations were merged into the **German Women's Enterprise**, which was led by Nazi, Gertrude Scholtz-Klink. Groups that refused to merge, were banned. Six million became members. The German Women's Enterprise made sure that women were exposed to all the latest Nazi teachings.
1935	The **Lebensborn** programme was introduced, which encouraged racial purity. Single women could have children by SS men and their children would be supported by the state.
1936	Women were banned from being lawyers and from serving on juries.
1937	The number of women at university dropped by two-thirds. Ideal womanhood was taught in schools. A shortage of workers meant that women were encouraged to go back to work. In industry, there was an introduction of a 'duty year' where women were allowed to work in factories for 'patriotic' reasons. The loan scheme introduced in 1933 was withdrawn.
1938	**Mother's Cross** was awarded to women with large families. Bronze = 4-5 children. Silver = 6-7. Gold for 8 or more. The Hitler Youth had to salute mothers wearing the cross. It was made easier to divorce women who could not have children.

Interpretation 5:

Despite propaganda about "more feminine women", the new priorities made it clear that obedience was the only trait that counted in women. Concern for keeping mothers in their homes lasted only as long as it was beneficial for the economy. Ultimately, it became obvious that the ideal Nazi woman learned flexibility rather than any specific skills so that she could leave the workplace and return to homemaking as the economy demanded.

Claudia Koonz, *Mothers in the Fatherland*

Interpretation 6:

Women appeared in the Nazi world view primarily as mothers — either as Aryan mothers, to be encouraged to have more children and to be made fit to do so by the new emphasis on physical training which the Nazis introduced in schools, workplaces and organisations such as the League of German Girls; or as 'inferior' mothers, as Jewish, gypsy, handicapped or other 'degenerate' mothers and potential mothers, to be discouraged or prevented from having children...

Charu Gupta, *Politics of Gender: Women in Nazi Germany*

How far do you agree with Interpretation 6 about Nazi attitudes towards the role of women?

Explain your answer, using both Interpretations, and your knowledge of the historical context. [20]

Your answer may include:

Points that agree with Interpretation 6:

- *Interpretation 6 suggests that the Nazi Party primarily valued Aryan women as mothers who could bring the next generation of 'racially pure' Nazis into the world.*
- *This agrees with my own knowledge that the birth rate dropped between 1930–33, and the Nazis introduced policies to encourage Aryan women to have children.*
- *The Mother's Cross was awarded to German women who had more than four children, and the Lebensborn programme supported unmarried mothers to have children with men from the SS. This shows the importance Nazis placed on motherhood and large families.*
- *Interpretation 6 states that the Nazi Party discouraged 'inferior' women from having children.*
- *This agrees with my own knowledge, for example, the Sterilisation Law allowed Jewish women to have an abortion, whereas it was not permitted for non-Jewish women.*

Points that disagree with Interpretation 6:

- *Interpretation 5 suggests that obedience was the most important trait that a German woman could have, and that German women were expected to do whatever the Nazi Party told them.*
- *This agrees with my own knowledge, as policies around motherhood weren't the only policies for women introduced by the Nazi Party.*
- *At first, women were encouraged to leave the workforce. For example, the Law for the Encouragement of Marriage paid women a loan if they gave up work, as Nazi ideology promoted the importance of women as homemakers.*
- *However, this stance was reversed in 1937, as a shortage of workers meant that women were actively encouraged to go back to work. For example, women were expected to do a 'duty year' in a factory as a patriotic gesture to the Nazi state.*
- *Women were expected to obediently follow Nazi guidance on what an 'ideal' German woman should look like. For example, they were expected to look neat and natural with tied back hair, no make-up, and modest clothes.*

This question should be marked in accordance with the levels-based mark scheme on page 62.

Make sure your answer to this question is in paragraphs and full sentences. Bullet points have been used in this example answer to suggest some information you could include.

NAZI AIMS AND POLICIES TOWARDS THE YOUNG

As the Nazis strengthened their hold on adult society, they did the same with the young. Hitler knew he needed the loyalty of young people, so that they would grow up to become devoted Nazis. Membership of Nazi youth groups increased from 107,000 in 1932 to 7.3 million in 1939.

The Hitler Youth

The **Hitler Youth** was for boys aged 14 and over. As well as promoting loyalty to the Nazi Party, it was a way to train future army leaders. It taught military skills, such as using weapons and map-reading, as well as Nazi ideology. It also organised camping trips and sporting activities to promote the Nazi ideals of being fit and healthy. Members of the Hitler Youth also swore an oath to report anyone who was disloyal, including parents.

The Hitler Youth membership was 55,000 in 1932 and rose to 568,000 in 1933. In 1936 the Nazis passed a law saying all young people had to belong to a youth organisation, so membership of the Hitler Youth grew even more.

The League of German Maidens

The **League of German Maidens** was the female equivalent of the Hitler Youth. It was a group for girls aged between 14–18. Girls were treated as equal to boys, but with a different set of aims and activities. They shared the same political training and indoctrination, including rallies and camping. Instead of military training, girls were taught household skills such as cooking, ironing, and sewing, and listened to lectures on topics such as 'Racial Hygiene for Marriage'.

A Hitler Youth parade c.1936.

BUND DEUTSCHER MÄDEL IN DER HITLER JUGEND

'League of German girls in the Hitler Youth'.

NAZI CONTROL OF THE YOUNG THROUGH EDUCATION

Nazi control extended to education. Previously, the curriculum was set by the local government. From 1934, it was centralised under Nazi control.

Teachers

Teachers had to take an oath of loyalty and join the **Nazi Teachers' League** and 97% of teachers joined. The League set out the ideals for teachers and ran courses about teaching in Nazi-approved ways. Children were encouraged to report teachers who did not conform. By 1936, 36% of teachers were members of the Nazi Party.

The school day

Lessons had to begin and end with a salute and 'Heil' to the Führer. Nazi posters and flags were prominently displayed. School radios broadcast political propaganda, and speeches by leaders were played to the school hall.

The curriculum

Nazi ideals were reinforced in every subject; Dolchstoss was taught in History, and the superiority of the Aryan race was taught in Biology. *Mein Kampf* was compulsory reading and only Nazi-approved textbooks were used from 1935.

Time for PE was doubled, and boxing was made compulsory for boys. Domestic science, including cooking and needlework, was compulsory for girls.

Source N:

We begin with the child when he is three years old. As soon as he begins to think, he gets a little flag put into his hand. Then he follows the school, the Hitler Youth, the SA and military training. We don't let him go. And then when adolescence is passed, then comes the Arbeitsfront [Labour Front], which takes him again and does not let him go until he dies, whether he likes it or not.

Robert Ley, Nazi Labour Front chief, 1938

Give **two** things you can infer from Source N about the Nazi control of the young. [4]

1. ***What I can infer:*** *The Nazis began to control the young from the very start of their education.* [1]

   Details in the source that tell me this: *It says 'We begin with the child when he is three years old'.* [1]

2. ***What I can infer:*** *Nazi youth programmes, such as the Hitler Youth, were compulsory.* [1]

   Details in the source that tell me this: *The source says the Nazi Party doesn't 'let him go'.* [1]

NAZI POLICIES TO REDUCE UNEMPLOYMENT

Tackling unemployment was vital to strengthening Germany's economy.

Employment under the Nazis

In 1933, six million Germans were unemployed, approximately 25% of the working-age population. By 1939, Nazi statistics claimed that unemployment had dropped to 0.5 million, approximately 2.5%. There were four main reasons for the reduction in unemployment.

1 National Labour Service (RAD)

Unemployed men were put to work building roads, drains, sports facilities and bridges. In 1933, this was voluntary, but by 1935 six months' service was compulsory for 18–25-year-old men.

➕ RAD gave work to 420,000 unemployed.

➖ RAD was unpopular with workers as it was badly paid and conditions in camps were poor.

Road construction workers in Germany in the 1930s

2 Autobahns

The Nazis planned to build 7000 km of motorways across Germany. The first opened in May 1935.

➕ The autobahn project reduced unemployment by 80,000.

➕ The new roads allowed for quicker transportation of military equipment.

➖ Spending on roads rose from 18 billion Marks to 37 billion between 1933 and 1938.

➖ Only 3000 km were completed by 1938.

A car drives down a new stretch of the Autobahn

3 Rearmament

The Nazis introduced conscription (compulsory military service) in 1935, which breached the terms of the Treaty of Versailles. The army had 1.4 million men by 1939. The increase in the size of the army led to a growth in heavy industries which created more jobs: coal and chemical production doubled, and oil, iron, and steel manufacturers trebled output between 1933 and 1939.

⊕ Conscription reduced unemployment by one million. An increase in employment in industry added to this.

⊕ Growth in the Aircraft industry reduced unemployment by nearly 70,000.

⊖ Spending on armaments rose from 3.5 billion Marks to 26 billion, 1933-39.

Construction underway on the infamous Hindenburg airship

4 Invisible unemployment

Data published by the Nazi government is often unreliable and false statistics were often used as propaganda. Some estimates suggest unemployment may really have been 1.75 million by 1939, rather than 0.5 million. This is partly due to invisible unemployment.

• Women and Jews were forced to give up work.

• Part-time work was counted as full time.

• Hundreds of thousands of people were hidden away in concentration camps and jails.

• Men working in RAD schemes or in jobs where unemployment was temporary (e.g. agriculture) were not included in the unemployment figures.

Prisoners at a concentration camp in 1938

CHANGES IN THE STANDARD OF LIVING

Some Germans experienced improvements in their quality of life but many did not.

Changes to jobs and wages

- There was an increase in jobs.
- Wages rose for those employed in key industries, like armaments.
- Farmers were protected by high prices for food.

- Jews were sacked and Jewish businesses suffered.
- Wages were poor for those in the RAD (National Labour Service).
- The cost of living rose.
- Average working hours rose from 43 to 49 hours per week.
- Workers didn't have the right to strike.

German Labour Front

The **German Labour Front** (**DAF** – see **page 31**) was established to control workers' rights, working hours and wages. It was led by Robert Ley. In 1933, there was a nationwide pay freeze, and this was enforced by the DAF.

Since all other trade unions had been banned, workers had nowhere else to turn. Any disruption of production could be punished by the DAF.

Strength Through Joy

The DAF set up **Strength Through Joy** (**KdF**) in 1933, which was a scheme to provide affordable leisure opportunities for workers, such as outings and tickets for sporting events and concerts.

⊕ By 1936, 35 million Germans were members.

⊕ By 1938, over 10 million had taken KdF holidays. It was even possible to win holidays.

Volkswagen (people's car)

In Nazi Germany, owning a car was only possible for the wealthy, so Hitler introduced a scheme where working-class Germans could save money towards a Volkswagen. Workers could buy a stamp for 5 Reichsmarks, and once they had 198 stamps, they could trade them in for a car. However, no one ever received a car. Instead, the money was channelled into the state.

Beauty of Labour

Beauty of Labour (**SdA**) was an offshoot of Strength Through Joy. It aimed to improve facilities for workers by providing canteens, lighting at work, showers, and toilets.

It gave tax breaks to companies to encourage improvements, and by 1938, 34,000 companies had enrolled in the scheme. However, workers were often expected to make the improvements themselves in their time off.

Explain why living standards rose under the Nazis between 1933 and 1939. You may use the following in your answer:

- Strength Through Joy (KdF)
- Beauty of Labour (SdA)

You must also use information of your own. [12]

Your answer may include:

Strength Through Joy:

- *The Strength Through Joy scheme (KdF) was set up by the Nazis in 1933 to improve the leisure options for workers. Among the options were affordable concerts, sporting events and holidays. There was huge uptake, with 36 million joining the programme by 1936.*

Beauty of Labour:

- *The Beauty of Labour (SdA) programme operated under Strength Through Joy and aimed to improve working conditions and facilities. This helped to improve workplaces by installing lighting, showers, and canteens.*

Decrease in unemployment:

- *The Nazis introduced schemes to help tackle the high levels of unemployment following the Great Depression. Nazi statistics suggests that unemployment fell from 6 million to 0.5 million.*
- *The RAD gave work to 420,000 unemployed people and improved public facilities by building roads and sports facilities.*
- *German rearmament also decreased unemployment by conscripting men into the armed forces, which also led to an increase in German heavy industry which created more jobs in steel and coal production. Those workers employed in rearmament and heavy industry also benefitted from an increase in wages.*

This question should be marked in accordance with the levels-based mark scheme on page 60.

Make sure your answer to this question is in paragraphs and full sentences. Bullet points have been used in this example answer to suggest some information you could include.

To get top marks, you need to include information other than the bullet points in the question.

NAZI RACIAL BELIEFS AND POLICIES

Hitler and the Nazi Party believed in the superiority of the Aryan race.

Nazi racial beliefs and policies

The Nazi Party promoted **Volksgemeinschaft**. This was the idea of a community of like-minded people working towards the same aims, who were healthy and racially pure. Hitler introduced policies which encouraged and promoted the growth of Volksgemeinschaft, while cleansing the population of any 'inferior' groups.

Herrenvolk and Aryans were the 'master race'. They were tall, blond haired and blue eyed.

Anything less was **Untermenschen**, or sub-human. This included **Slavic** people from Eastern Europe.

Jews and Sinti-Roma '**gypsies**' were deemed **Lebensunwortes** meaning 'unworthy of life'.

Being Jewish was seen as a race (rather than a religion), so Jewish blood could not be 'pure' in Nazi ideology.

Eugenics

Nazis believed in **eugenics**. They wanted to improve the genetic quality of the German population.

One element of this was selective breeding which encouraged Germans with desirable features to reproduce, for example the Lebensborn programme (see **page 44**).

Racial hygiene

Racial hygiene was one step further than eugenics. Hitler wanted Germany to be populated only by members of the Aryan race, or as close to it as possible. In 1935, the Party banned inter-racial marriage and sex.

A Lebensborn nursing home where the wives and girlfriends of SS members could get assistance following the birth of a child.

TREATMENT OF MINORITIES

Slavs

Slavs were found across Eastern Europe in Eastern Germany, Poland, Russia, and the Balkans. They lived in the space Hitler felt the German Reich needed to move into known as 'Lebensraum'.

They were persecuted in the 1930s for being **Untermenschen**.

Sinti-Roma/Gypsies

The Sinti-Roma population was around 26,000 in Germany in the 1930s. Their nomadic life and different culture meant they were described as 'work shy'. They were deemed **Lebensunwortes** and a threat to racial purity. They were persecuted from 1935 onwards.

1936	Sinti-Roma were moved out of Berlin for the Olympics. Some to Dachau concentration camp, 600 to Marzahn, a labour camp outside Berlin, where they only had two toilets, three water taps and no electricity.
1938	Travelling in groups was banned. This was a direct attack on Sinti-Roma culture. Citizenship was removed from those who failed to settle or to pay taxes.
1939	Plans were drawn up for deportation.

Homosexuals

Homosexuality was illegal before the Nazis came to power, but laws were tightened, and persecution rose under the Nazis. Gay people were excluded from Volksgemeinschaft.

Gay men were deemed to be dangerous for the race programmes, for the strength of the army and were linked to the 'depravity' of the Weimar era.

Voluntary castration was promoted. Many were sent to concentration camps, where they were particularly badly beaten. Some estimates suggest that around 5,000 died in the camps.

People with disabilities

Physical and mental disabilities were against the Nazi ideal of a strong master race, so anyone with a disability was also excluded from Volksgemeinschaft.

In 1933, the **Law for the Prevention of Hereditarily Diseased Offspring** was passed. Sterilisation was made compulsory for those who were mentally ill, physically deformed, deaf or blind. Approximately 400,000 people were sterilised by 1939.

THE PERSECUTION OF THE JEWS

Despite forming less than 1% of the German population, Jews were mercilessly persecuted by the policies of the Nazis.

Persecution of the Jews

1st April 1933

The SA organised a national boycott of Jewish-owned shops. It was said to be 'un-German' to use Jewish businesses. The Star of David was crudely painted on shop windows, along with the word 'Jude' (Jew).

April 1933

Jews were banned from working in government jobs and those in the civil service and teaching were sacked. Schools were forbidden to have more than 1.5% of Jews in the student body.

September 1933

Jews had to provide Aryan heritage back to 1800 to be able to inherit land. This was impossible, so Jewish families lost land.

1934

Many parks, swimming pools and sports clubs refused entry to Jews. Jewish students were banned from professional exams such as dentistry and law.

May 1935

Jews were banned from joining the army.

The founder of communism, Karl Marx, was Jewish so Jews became linked to communist conspiracies as well. Nazis and other right-wing groups also blamed the Jews for defeat in the war and for the Weimar 'betrayal'.

The Nuremberg Laws

On 15th September 1935, **The Nuremberg Laws** were announced at a Nazi rally.

Reich Citizenship Law removed citizenship and civil rights for Jews. Removed from the Volksgemeinschaft, Jews could no longer hold a passport or vote. They were no longer 'citizens', but 'subjects', of the Reich. Jews had to sew on a yellow Star of David to their clothes.

Reich Law for the Protection of German Blood and Honour prevented inter-racial marriage and sex. Jews could be imprisoned for a breach.

Events of Kristallnacht

In November 1938, events led up to **Kristallnacht** (Night of the Broken Glass).

7ᵗʰ November

A Polish Jew, shot and wounded a Nazi diplomat, Ernst vom Rath, in the German Embassy in Paris. This sparked a furious backlash on Jews across Germany.

8ᵗʰ November

Hitler and Goebbels ordered Hanover newspapers to publish a condemnation of the shooting.

9ᵗʰ November

Vom Rath died of his wounds. Outraged, Goebbels ordered punishment squads of SA and SS to attack Jewish buildings, including synagogues. The SA were told not to wear uniforms, to make it appear as though local people were carrying out the attacks.

The police were told not to intervene. The fire service was told only to put out the flames in non-Jewish buildings. Meanwhile, the SS rounded up Jews.

814 shops, 171 homes and 191 synagogues were destroyed according to Nazi newspapers. 30,000 Jews were arrested and 91 lost their lives on Kristallnacht.

Windows of a Jewish business smashed during Kristallnacht

Most of the German population remained silent, while some openly supported the persecution of the Jews.

Events of Kristallnacht

Kristallnacht marked a turning point in the severity of Jewish persecution, as Jews were treated even more brutally afterwards. Jews were blamed for the trouble, and Hitler demanded that Jews across Germany be punished.

- 20,000 men were sent to concentration camps.
- No insurance was paid to Jews for the damage to their homes and businesses.
- No business could reopen under Jewish management.
- Jewish children were banned from schools.

January 1939

The Reich Office for Jewish Emigration was established. It aimed to deport all Jews. Many left of their own accord, some estimates suggest 250,000 fled.

Explain why there was persecution of minorities under the Nazi Party 1933-39. You may use the following in your answer:

- Nazi beliefs about race
- the Nuremberg Laws

You **must** also use information of your own. [12]

Your answer may include:

Nazi beliefs about race:

- *The Nazi Party believed in Volksgemeinschaft and the superiority of the Aryan race. Anyone who did not belong to Volksgemeinschaft or possess Aryan characteristics could be persecuted. This included Jews, Slavs, Sinti-Roma, homosexuals, and people with physical or mental disabilities.*
- *Hitler's personal ideas about race were influential to the persecution of minorities. He had established some of his views on race in Mein Kampf, and he used the Nazi Party to turn these ideas into a reality.*
- *Nazis wanted to use eugenics and policies of racial purity to prevent 'pure' Germans from marrying and having children with 'inferior' people. One way they did this was with the Law for the Prevention of Hereditarily Diseased Offspring. This made it legal to sterilise anyone who had a physical or mental illness to prevent them from having children. Approximately 400,000 people were sterilised under the Nazi regime.*

The Nuremberg Laws:

- *The Nuremberg Laws openly discriminated against Jewish people. The laws removed citizenship and civil rights for Jews. This meant that Jewish people were vulnerable to even greater persecution from the Nazi state as well the German public.*

Kristallnacht:

- *The Nazi Party used the death of vom Rath to legitimise more attacks on Jewish people. Following Kristallnacht, Jewish businesses were forced to close and Jewish children were banned from school.*

Lack of resistance:

- *The Nazi Party was able to increase its persecution of minorities because there was a lack of resistance from the German population. Some Germans who opposed the discrimination may have been too afraid to speak out, fearful of being sent to a concentration camp or executed.*
- *Hitler had made no secret of his hatred for Jews, and the German public had voted him into power despite this. This suggests that some Germans agreed with the persecution because they also held antisemitic beliefs.*
- *Anti-Jewish sentiment was spread using film, posters and in schools, so many Germans were encouraged to believe that Jews should be persecuted, and the discriminatory laws seemed to legalise Nazi persecution.*

This question should be marked in accordance with the levels-based mark scheme on page 60.

Make sure your answer to this question is in paragraphs and full sentences. Bullet points have been used in this example answer to suggest some information you could include.

To get top marks, you need to include information other than the bullet points in the question.

EXAMINATION PRACTICE

1. Give **two** things you can infer from Source A about the Kapp Putsch. [4]

2. Explain why the Nazi Party had limited success in the period 1923–29.

    You may use the following in your answer:

    *   the Weimar Government's foreign policy
    *   the Munich Putsch

    You **must** also use information of your own. [12]

Source B:

A poster from 1936. The text in the top left says: "The Nazi Party secures the Volksgemeinshaft.

3. Study sources B and C.

    (a) How useful are sources B and C for an enquiry into Nazi use of propaganda? [8]

    ### Interpretation 1

    'Leni Riefenstahl was commissioned to make a detailed record of mass rallies, festival, speeches and the 1936 Olympic Games. The results were probably the most impressive propaganda films ever made, one of which was 'Triumph of the Will'... films were also used to put across racial values and ideas. The principles of eugenics and racial breeding were explained by making comparisons with crops and animals. Above all, the cinema became a powerful weapon in stirring up hatred against Jewish people in Germany.'

    From *'Weimar and Nazi Germany'*, by Stephen Lee, 1996.

    ### Interpretation 2

    'Nazi propaganda and indoctrination appears to have been most successful when it was aimed at the young, whose opinions were not yet strongly formed, or when their messages overlapped with the traditional values of particular groups....Anti-Semitism and nationalist resentment of the Treaty of Versailles ran through all classes and the Nazis were able to reinforce these attitudes through their propaganda. Thus Nazi propaganda was most successful when it built upon existing beliefs and values. Where Nazi propaganda challenged deeply held beliefs, such as religion, it was less successful'

    From *'Democracy and Nazism'*, by Robert Whitfield, 2015.

    (b) Study Interpretations 1 and 2. They give different views about the Nazi use of propaganda. What is the main difference between these views? Explain your answer using details from both interpretations. [4]

    (c) Suggest **one** reason why Interpretations 1 and 2 give different views about the Nazi use of propaganda.
        You may use sources B and C on page 57 to help explain your answer. [4]

    (d) How far do you agree with Interpretation 2 about the Nazi use of propaganda?

        Explain your answer, using both interpretations and your knowledge of the historical context.
        [16 for content + 4 for SPaG = 20]

EXAMINATION PRACTICE ANSWERS

1 **What I can infer:** I can infer that some people thought the leaders of the Putsch weren't thinking straight or behaving rationally.
   Details in the source that tell me this: The source says the Putsch is 'absurd' and is not the result of sensible policy.
   What I can infer: I can infer that the Kapp Putsch could lead to violence and death.
   Details in the source that tell me this: The text says, "Enough blood has flowed since 1914." This suggests that more blood might flow.   [4]

2 Your answer may include:

   During the 1920s, the Weimar Government had a successful foreign policy which helped to kick-start industry and improve relationships abroad. This meant that voters across all social classes were satisfied with the Weimar Government and didn't want to support extreme political parties. The Dawes Plan and the Young plan helped to reduce reparations and agree a more sensible timeline for payments. The Dawes Plan also led to a £40 million loan from the USA which was invested in industry. American investment was popular with the working-classes because it provided more employment, and it was popular with the upper- and middle-classes because it improved confidence in Germany's economy and improved her reputation abroad.

   The Munich Putsch showed that there was limited support for the Nazi Party. Although the Nazis had been gaining popularity, they failed to overthrow the Government in Munich. This was significant because following Hitler's arrest in November 1923, the Nazi Party was banned until 1925, and Hitler was imprisoned for 9 months. This caused disruption and meant that the Nazi Party was a limited threat in the early 1920s. The failure of the Munich Putsch also showed to Hitler that he was unable to overthrow the Weimar Government using force, and that he needed to focus on becoming electable instead.

   Another reason why there was limited support for the Nazi Party in the period 1923-29 is because the German public saw an increase in their freedoms and quality of life following World War One, so certain groups, such as young people, were content with the Weimar Government. For example, the Weimar Constitution gave women more rights, including the right to vote, equal rights to men and the right to stand in elections. There was also a boom in cultural movements, such as cinema, nightlife, and music.   [12]

3 (a) Source B shows that the Nazi Party used propaganda to promote their belief that Aryan people belonged to the Volksgemeinschaft. This agrees with my own knowledge that the Aryan race was seen as 'superior', and that non-Aryans were excluded the Volksgemeinschaft. This poster also shows a family with multiple children. This agrees with my own knowledge that the Nazi Party used propaganda to promote the importance of 'racially pure' Germans having large families, as during the 1930s, the Nazi Party wanted to increase Germany's birth rate. This poster was produced by the NSDAP so is an accurate reflection of Nazi Party propaganda at the time. Because it is an illustration, rather than a photograph, it shows the NSDAP's depiction of the ideal German family. However, it is limited because it doesn't include information of other Nazi ideologies at the time, for example, the persecution of minorities. Furthermore, posters were only one example of propaganda, and I know that the Nazis also used cinema, radio, and the press to promote their ideologies.

       Source C shows that Hitler thought the theatre, art, literature, cinema, press and posters could all be used as propaganda. This agrees with my knowledge that the Nazi Party used all these formats to spread Nazi ideology, for example the Great German Art Exhibition was used to showcase Nazi-approved artworks. The source also suggests that Hitler thought that propaganda was particularly effective on the young. This reinforces my knowledge that Hitler used education in schools to spread Nazi ideology, for example, *Mein Kampf* was compulsory reading. This source is useful because it is a direct quote from Hitler, and he was the leader, and therefore most influential member, of the Nazi Party. However, *Mein Kampf* was written before Hitler became the leader of Germany, so his opinions may have changed later in his career. Furthermore, Goebbels was the Nazi Minister for Propaganda, and this source does not mention him, so we don't know whether this source agrees with Goebbels' opinions on propaganda.   [8]

   (b) A main difference is that Interpretation 1 suggests that the Nazis used cinema to promote the persecution of minorities, by "stirring up hatred against Jewish people". On the other hand, Interpretation 2 suggests that the German people already held antisemitic beliefs which "ran through all classes", and that propaganda merely reinforced beliefs that already existed.   [4]

   (c) The Interpretations might differ because they have chosen to place an emphasis on different details. Interpretation 1 is focussed on the role of cinema in promoting Nazi ideology, whereas Interpretation 2 suggests that it wasn't the medium that mattered, but the person who was exposed to the propaganda. Source B supports Interpretation 2, because traditional family values would have been deeply held beliefs amongst many Germans. Source A helps to support Interpretation 1, as Hitler himself thought that cinema was an important tool for political control.   [4]

   (d) Interpretation 2 states that Nazi propaganda was most effective when it was aimed at young people. The growth in Nazi youth programmes, such as the Hitler Youth and the League of German Maidens would suggest that Nazi propaganda was effective in recruiting young people. Membership of Nazi youth groups grew from about 107,000 in 1932, to 7.3 million in 1939. However, by 1936 it was effectively compulsory for boys to join the Hitler Youth, so propaganda wasn't entirely responsible for the rise in membership. Furthermore, there was some youth opposition to the Nazi Party from groups like the Swing Kids and the Edelweiss Pirates, which would suggest that Nazi propaganda didn't always work on the young.

Interpretation 2 also says that propaganda was also effective when it reinforced existing beliefs. For example, some German people held antisemitic beliefs prior to the formation of the Nazi Party by believing in 'stab in the back' theories that blamed Jews for Germany's defeat in World War One. These beliefs were reinforced using propaganda, for example the Nazi film *The Eternal Jew*, suggested that Jewish people were like rats who spread diseases. Films such as these would have encouraged people to discriminate against the Jewish population. However, it was not just propaganda that influenced people's beliefs. Fear of repercussions would have also prevented people who disagreed with the Nazi Party from speaking out against propaganda. The Nazi Party used violent methods, such as the Gestapo, concentration camps and the threat of executions, to stamp out anyone who disagreed with Nazi ideology.

Interpretation 2 also states that Nazi propaganda was less effective in certain areas, such as religion. This agrees with my own knowledge that the Reich Church (the church created by the Nazi Party) had limited success, and only about 25% of churches became Reich Churches. This can be interpretated as propaganda having a limited impact on deeply held beliefs. However, there was organised opposition to the Nazi Party's policies on religion from the Confessing Church, and their stance against Nazi interference in religion may have been the reason why propaganda was less effective in challenging religious beliefs.

Overall, although I agree that Nazi propaganda was more effective when it was used to reinforce existing beliefs, rather than changing people's minds, I also believe that propaganda wasn't the only tool used by the Nazis to encourage people to conform to Nazi Party ideology. Fear of the repercussions of speaking out or disobeying the Nazi Party was also instrumental in reinforcing Nazi beliefs.   [16]

LEVELS-BASED MARK SCHEMES FOR EXTENDED RESPONSE QUESTIONS

Questions 2, 3(a), 3(b), 3(c) and 3(d) require extended writing and use mark bands. Each answer will be assessed against the mark bands, and a mark is awarded based on the mark band it fits into.

The descriptors have been written in simple language to give an indication of the expectations of each mark band. See the Edexcel website for the official mark schemes used.

Question 2

Level 4 **(10-12 marks)**	• The answer gives an analytical explanation which is focussed on the question. • The answer is well developed, coherent and logically structured. • The information given is accurate and relevant to the question. • The answer shows excellent knowledge and understanding of the period. • The answer includes information that goes beyond the stimulus points in the question.
Level 3 **(7-9 marks)**	• The answer shows some analysis which is generally focussed on the question. • The answer is mostly coherent and logically structured. • Most of the information given is accurate and relevant to the question. • The answer shows good knowledge and understanding of the period.
Level 2 **(4-6 marks)**	• The answer shows limited analysis, and not all points are justified. • The answer shows some organisation, but the reasoning is not sustained. • Some accurate and relevant information is given. • The answer shows some knowledge and understanding of the period.
Level 1 **(1-3 marks)**	• A simple or general answer is given. • The answer lacks development or organisation. • The answer shows limited knowledge and understanding of the period.
0 marks	• No answer has been given or the answer given makes no relevant points.

Question 3 (a)

Level 3 (6-8 marks)	• The answer gives a sophisticated judgement on how useful the sources are. • The answer is supported and developed with valid information about the content of the sources and their provenance, and how this affects the sources' usefulness. • The answer interprets the sources using historical context and evaluates how this affects the sources' usefulness.
Level 2 (3-5 marks)	• The answer gives a judgement on how useful the sources are. • The answer contains some information about the content of the sources and their provenance, and how this affects the sources' usefulness. • The answer gives information about the historical context of the sources, and how this affects the sources' usefulness.
Level 1 (1-2 marks)	• The answer gives a simple judgement on how useful the sources are. • The answer contains undeveloped information about the content of the sources and their provenance. • The answer gives limited information about the historical context of the sources.
0 marks	• No answer has been given or the answer given makes no relevant points.

Question 3 (b)

Level 2 (3-4 marks)	• The answer interprets the sources and gives a key difference with supporting information.
Level 1 (1-2 marks)	• The answer gives a limited interpretation of the sources, with paraphrased or extracted information, or no supporting evidence.
0 marks	• No answer has been given or the answer given makes no relevant points.

Question 3 (c)

Level 2 (3-4 marks)	• The answer explains why the sources have different interpretations. • The answer is justified with accurate and relevant information.
Level 1 (1-2 marks)	• The answer gives a simple explanation why the sources have different interpretations. • The answer shows limited or undeveloped justification.
0 marks	• No answer has been given or the answer given makes no relevant points.

Question 3 (d)

Level 4 (13-16 marks)	• The answer gives an explained evaluation, considers alternative views and comes to a justified judgement. • The interpretations have been analysed carefully, and the answer communicates how the different views have been conveyed. • The answer includes relevant and accurate knowledge. • The overall judgement is justified, and the reasoning is coherent and logically structured.
Level 3 (9-12 marks)	• The answer gives an explained evaluation and agrees or disagrees with the interpretation. • The answer shows good analysis of the interpretations and uses their different views to support the evaluation. • The answer includes relevant and accurate knowledge. • An overall judgement is given with some justification, and the reasoning is generally sustained.
Level 2 (5-8 marks)	• The answer offers a valid evaluation and agrees or disagrees with the interpretation. • The answer shows some analysis and selection of details from the interpretations. • Some relevant knowledge is used to support the answer. • An overall judgement is given but it is limited or undeveloped.
Level 1 (1-4 marks)	• A simple answer is given. • The answer lacks analysis of the interpretations or includes paraphrasing or direct quotation. • The answer shows generalised knowledge.
0 marks	• No answer has been given or the answer given makes no relevant points.

Question 3(d) — SPaG (Spelling, Punctuation and Grammar)

High Level (4 marks)	• The answer is consistently spelled and punctuated correctly. • The answer uses grammar correctly and effectively. • The answer includes a wide range of specialist terms, where appropriate.
Intermediate (2-3 marks)	• The answer is largely spelled and punctuated correctly. • The answer uses grammar correctly. • The answer includes a good range of specialist terms, where appropriate.
Threshold (1 mark)	• The answer shows a reasonable level of correct spelling and punctuation. • The answer shows some control of grammar, and errors do not hinder meaning. • The answer includes a limited range of specialist terms, where appropriate.
0 marks	• No answer is given, or the answer does not relate to the question. • The answer does not meet the threshold performance level, and errors severely hinder meaning.

INDEX

EXAMINATION TIPS

With your examination practice, use a boundary approximation using the following table. These boundaries have been calculated as an average across past History papers rather than an average of this paper. Be aware that the grade boundaries can vary quite a lot from year to year, so they should be used as a guide only.

Grade	9	8	7	6	5	4	3	2	1
Boundary	83%	75%	67%	58%	51%	42%	30%	19%	8%

1. Read the questions carefully. Don't give an answer to a question that you *think* is appearing (or wish was appearing!) rather than the actual question.

2. Make sure your handwriting is legible. The examiner can't award you marks if they can't read what you've written.

3. Make sure that you revise all the course content. All the questions are compulsory, so you need to be prepared to answer them.

4. Learn topic-specific vocabulary and make sure you're comfortable using it.

5. Don't spend too long on the 4-mark questions.

6. Try to back up your points with evidence wherever possible.

7. When asked to make inferences in question 1, make sure your inferences are relevant to the question.

8. To get top marks in Q2, you need to include information beyond what is provided in the bullet points.

9. To do well in Q3(a) make sure to link the provenance to the content of the sources.

10. It's helpful to think of all the sub questions for Q3 as part of the same enquiry, all leading towards the final analysis in Q3(d).

11. In the longer written questions, use linking words and phrases to show you are developing your points or comparing information, for example, "as a consequence", "this shows that" and "on the other hand". This shows the examiner that you're able to analyse, evaluate and judge historical events.

12. If you need extra paper, make sure you clearly signal that your answer is continued elsewhere. Remember that longer answers don't necessarily score more highly than shorter, more concise answers.

Good luck!

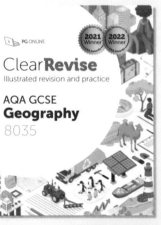

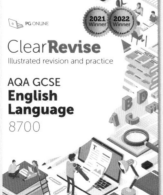

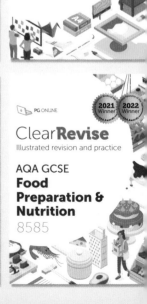